The Peppercorn Tree

I0369377

John T Fitzgibbon

First published by Busybird Publishing 2023

Copyright © 2023 John T Fitzgibbon

ISBN:
Paperback: 978-1-922954-72-5
Ebook: 978-1-922954-73-2

This work is copyright. Apart from any use permitted under the *Copyright Act 1968*, no part of this publication may be reproduced, stored in a retrieval system or transmitted in any form or by any means, electronic, mechanical, photocopying, recording or otherwise, without the prior written permission of John T Fitzgibbon.

The information in this book is based on the author's experiences and opinions. The author and publisher disclaim responsibility for any adverse consequences, which may result from use of the information contained herein. Permission to use any external content has been sought by the author. Any breaches will be rectified in further editions of the book.

Cover Image: Maryam Homaei

Cover design: Busybird Publishing

Layout and typesetting: Busybird Publishing

Busybird Publishing
2/118 Para Road
Montmorency, Victoria
Australia 3094
www.busybird.com.au

TABLE OF CONTENTS

ACKNOWLEDGEMENTS	i
FOREWORD: HEROES OF A LOST CAUSE	iii
INTRODUCTION	vii

CHAPTER ONE
FIRST DAY OF SCHOOL — 1

CHAPTER TWO
THE FIRES OF HELL — 8

CHAPTER THREE
SISTER BARNARD — 19

CHAPTER FOUR
MY JOURNAL — 30

CHAPTER FIVE
RUNNING AWAY — 36

CHAPTER SIX
A NEW FRIEND — 42

CHAPTER SEVEN
STANDING UP FOR MYSELF — 51

CHAPTER EIGHT
GOODBYE FRIEND, GOODBYE SCHOOL — 58

CHAPTER NINE
BECOMING A MAN — 67

CHAPTER TEN
PANDORA'S BOX — 75

CHAPTER ELEVEN
THE HEALING PROCESS — 83

CHAPTER TWELVE
THE APOLOGY — 98

CHAPTER THIRTEEN
FRUSTRATION — 105

CHAPTER FOURTEEN
GETTING ON WITH LIFE — 109

ACKNOWLEDGEMENTS

I would like to acknowledge these people in the order they appear as my story unfolds in this book.

First is Judy, whom I met on the riverbank. I owe this woman my life. If it wasn't for her, I'm sure I wouldn't be here today, and my story would never have been told. I also owe her for reading me all those books; I learnt more from Judy than I learnt at school.

The second person is Denis Ryan, for getting me started on the right track by introducing me to Broken Rites. Without him and that connection, I would still be looking for the right help. Denis's relentless fight for justice makes him a hero in my eyes. After being treated appallingly by Victoria Police and ostracised by many within the Mildura community, he was eventually vindicated and made a Member of the Order of Australia, Mildura Citizen of the Year, and Freeman of the City of Mildura. Perhaps most importantly for Denis, in 2016 Chief Commissioner Graham Ashton offered an apology to him on behalf of Victoria Police. A similar apology was provided by the Police Association of Victoria. Denis's book *Unholy Trinity* chronicles the battles he faced in trying to uncover the hideous activities of Father Day. Today, I am proud to call Denis a friend.

Thirdly, I thank Dr Bernard Barrett, PhD, for the many emails of support and assistance. He did his best to find the right psychologist for me, and introduced me to Towards Healing.

Next, I don't know how to adequately thank Kerry Buchecker from Towards Healing. She is a very understanding and kind woman who constantly patched me up and put me on the right track.

I owe these people so much. A sincere thank-you to all of you.

It would be remiss of me not to mention some other people whom I've never met, and who didn't help me personally but had a huge impact on bringing institutional childhood abuse to light in Australia. Chrissie Foster and her late husband, Anthony, became high-profile advocates after discovering two of their daughters had been abused by a Catholic priest. Chrissie has written two books about her experiences battling the Church, dealing with the trauma of losing one daughter from a drug overdose, caring for the other who has required full-time care since being hit by a car, and continuing her advocacy after the death of Anthony. Her books are called *Hell on the Way to Heaven* and *Still Standing*. Then there is Julia Gillard who, as prime minister, stared down the institutions and established the Royal Commission into Institutional Responses to Child Sexual Abuse. These three are also heroes to the cause.

Finally, thanks to Nicolas Brasch for his assistance in getting this book written and published.

Note: Three names in this book have been changed: one for privacy reasons; the others because my memory isn't what it once was, and I cannot be certain of their real names. Nevertheless, everything related to these people is as it happened.

I have also chosen not to include a photo of Father Day in this book. There are plenty on newspaper files and in other books. But he has contaminated my life enough.

FOREWORD:

HEROES OF A LOST CAUSE

BY ALI CUPPER

It is my great honour to contribute some words to this book about my friend, John Fitzgibbon.

I first met John in 2019 not long after I had become Mildura's state MP, but by then I had admired him for many years.

It all started during a drinking session at the Workers in the early 2010s. I was having a beer with a friend and his friend (whom I didn't know very well). I had just got back from the bar when they were deep in conversation about 'Monsignor Day'. The name sounded vaguely familiar but I couldn't quite place it … It was lost on me.

'What's Monsignor Day?' I asked, thinking it was a type of *day*, like Crazy Hair Day or Taco Tuesday.

My friend looked at me and said, 'He was a paedophile priest.'

'Oh okay, sorry, I thought you meant a day … as in a *day*, like … never mind.'

I kept listening. The friend of a friend was from a large local Catholic family. She would have been born in the 1970s and probably too young to remember Monsignor Day. But her parents would have known him.

At the time I was a local activist, railing against a local political culture which (in my opinion) stifled debate to protect the conservative, political status quo. I loved a good yarn about speaking truth the power. And boy had I come to the right place … so I started asking questions.

My grandmother came from a Catholic family, but as far as I could tell she hadn't been practicing since she was a kid. I asked Dad if he knew anything. He remembered when he was at Mildura Tech in the late 1960s, some kids would rib each other about being 'got at' by the local priest, but he didn't really know what they were talking about.

On the other hand, I had a friend whose family was much closer to the action. His mother had grown up in Mildura in a big Catholic family.

I asked him about Monsignor Day. He gave me a basic crash course. He talked about the Ballarat diocese, the local media, clerk of courts, and Detective Sergeant Barritt. He also told me about the great man, Denis Ryan.

He said that when his mother was a teenager, a friend of hers was molested by Monsignor Day. My friend's mother worked up the courage to disclose it to her own mother. The response? She was kicked out of home for lying.

If not for the kindness of the local nuns, my best friend's mum would have been homeless. My friend wondered what those nuns knew, but didn't say.

The crimes in themselves were horrifying. But something else was equally stark. The climate that made it thrive. The stoic culture of silence – of keeping your head down and not questioning authority.

Monsignor Day was the apex villain of the story. But the culture of silence was a close second. Without it, he wouldn't have lasted five minutes.

I spoke to my friend, Graeme O'Neil, a local journalist of the baby boomer generation. He was a young cadet journalist at the *Sunraysia Daily* in the 1960s and the thing he found most startling was that this scourge of child sexual abuse and the protection racket that surrounded it wasn't a secret – it was common knowledge.

So many people knew, but they did nothing.

It was around that time, in 2013, that Denis Ryan's book, *Unholy Trinity*, was published. My best friend read it before I did. 'It's just weird reading this unbelievable cop story and seeing all the local references, like Eleventh Street!' he said.

He lent me his copy and I read the whole thing overnight.

Since 2013, the Catholic Church – and other faith-based institutions – have been forced to answer for their cruelty and hypocrisy. But as recently as a few months ago, I heard an employee for a Catholic agency refer to children who were 'trespassed' by the Church. It made me angry. 'Trespassed? What? Like walking on land without an easement? For fuck's sake, those kids were *raped*. Fucking SAY IT!!'

The softening of the language felt to me like a softening of the truth.

When members of the Catholic Church hear about the crimes of the clergy, their faith provides a cushion for the rage. But I have no cushion, so when I read *Unholy Trinity*, it was metal on metal. After turning the final page, I was boiling. The book ended, not with literary prose, but with three jarring witness statements from three primary victims. One of them was John Fitzgibbon.

I imagined that little boy. Alone and terrified. Completely bewildered about what was happening to him and why. Preyed upon by a sadist, drunk on power, and somehow – unfathomably – protected by society.

An article appeared in my newsfeed about a former child rape victim burning down a Catholic Church in Europe. Impulsively, in a fit of righteous anger, I shared it, along with a spray of disparaging comments about the legacy of the local Catholic Church.

I was strongly criticised for it and rightly so. It was a bit much. I received a complaint letter from the local priest. He made some reasonable points. But his suggestion that I have a think about the 'benevolent' things that John Day did, such as building a local primary school, made me vomit in my mouth.

In 2017, I was running a local program called the Australian Advocacy and Politics Summer School (AAPSS). One of the sessions explored the power of institutions like the Catholic Church and the political will to challenge it.

In the audience that day were a number of baby boomers who grew up in the local Catholic Church, some of whom were teenagers at St Joseph's College when Monsignor Day was moralising about bikinis by day, and raping children ... also by day. The mix of anger and grief was palpable. A significant amount of that anger was directed at one of the speakers, Victorian MP Fiona Patten, who far from being an enemy of the good fight, had lobbied tirelessly for the Royal Commission into Institutional Responses to Child Sexual Abuse.

I couldn't help but wonder if the anger they were projecting at her might well have been anger at themselves – or their families – as they reckoned with their own experiences and decisions at the time. Fiona was an easy target.

On that day, a late apology had been Denis Ryan. He was undisputedly a hero of the cause to run Monsignor Day out of town, and ultimately bring justice and recognition to the countless children he raped and assaulted.

But he was not the only hero.

Among the others stood John Fitzgibbon. As a little boy he was confused about why he was summoned to Monsignor Day's office for being naughty. He had thought that he was a good boy. It is hard to fathom how confused he must have been. Confused and terrified. A childhood stolen and a future irreparably changed.

There would have been a million cultural forces keeping John silent. Sexual abuse is uniquely hard to disclose. Abusers know that, and exploit it.

But John spoke the truth. He stared down the social forces, the inner demons and the ghost of that monstrous sadist, John Day. He spoke the truth about what happened to him. In doing so, he gave a voice to all the other adult survivors of Day's crimes. When hope was lost, he found it, and gave it to others.

Being asked to write about my admiration for John is a frustrating exercise, because ultimately I have no words. Just love, and a respect bordering on awe.

Thank you for your example, John. It is an honour to know you.

INTRODUCTION

On 22 February 2008, I received an apology from the Catholic Church for the sexual abuse I suffered from Father (later Monsignor) John Day when I was a child. It had taken more than fifty years for this apology and admission. Fifty years in which I kept the secret to myself. Fifty years of nightmares. Fifty years of depression. Fifty years of hell.

All that time I felt alone, but I now know, as we all do, that I was not alone. Thousands of children were abused by people in authority. Not just in the Catholic Church – indeed, not just in religious institutions, but in all sorts of places by all sorts of people.

Every one of these victims of abuse have their own story to tell. Tragically, many took their own lives and their stories died with them. This is my story. It's no more important than anyone else's; no more horrific than anyone else's. But it's my story and now, after more than five decades, I have to tell it.

I feel my pain, I feel my anger.
I feel my loss of a child within me.
I cannot tell, I cannot speak.
I have no face, nightmares of horror still haunt me.
I cannot cry, my soul is crippled, and my hope is gone.
I can't get out, the hole is dark, or is it the hole within me?
I feel I am in an ocean with the ups and downs.
I think I am going mad.
I would like to feel others' pain, but I am too numb to feel my own.
I've got no love within me, it's been taken away.
I have no trust, I have no beliefs, it's just dark out there.
I have a lump in my throat, it won't go away.

I should move on from the past, but it won't let me go.
My nerves are shot, why I am I still here? I've tried but it doesn't work.
Is there a heaven? I hope not because the priests will be there.

– Written by me in grade seven at the age of
thirteen, two days before I walked out of school,
never to return.

CHAPTER ONE

FIRST DAY OF SCHOOL

I woke to a rap on my bedroom door and the shriek of my sister, Marlene. 'Time for school,' she yelled.

I leapt out of bed, as excited as I had ever been before. It was the end of January 1952, I was four years and three months old, and today was my first day of school. Who wouldn't be excited?

Mum had laid my new school clothes out on the dresser the night before, and my sparkling new school shoes and pristine school bag stood proudly against the squat feet of the dresser.

I couldn't get dressed fast enough. I had heard so much about school, and whenever well-meaning family members told me not to be nervous, I couldn't help wondering what on earth they were talking about. Nervous? Not on your nelly. I was going to learn new things and make new friends. Why would anyone be nervous?

I raced out of my room with my shirt buttoned crookedly, my shoes on the wrong feet, and the intoxicating smell of leather from the strap of my school bag wafting into my nostrils.

I could barely stand still as Mum fidgeted with my shirt buttons, rearranged and tied my shoes, and straightened up a few other loose ends.

'Let's go,' I said.

'One minute young man,' she said. 'You have to have breakfast first.'

'I'll miss the bus. I can't miss the bus.'

'We've got plenty of time. Eat your breakfast and then we can go.'

The bus stop was about a mile from home. As I gobbled down my breakfast, I could see out the window to our land, which was nothing less than a boy's paradise. On one side of the house was bushland, with a channel running through it; on another were grape vines; and the other our animals. Mum had a couple of Jersey cows and about two hundred chooks. Every few days I took eggs and milk across the road to an elderly Italian couple, and they gave me home-grown vegetables in return.

We were surrounded by farmers, most of whom used Clydesdales instead of tractors. Good tractors cost a fair bit and so most people around us could only afford cheap ones. These were so unreliable that the farmers reckoned it took two hours to get their tractor going in the morning, and only an hour to get a Clydesdale into its working gear. We didn't have a tractor. we didn't even have a car at that stage, so we walked everywhere or caught the bus. The walk to the bus stop on that first school morning was a very familiar one for me.

Mum didn't come to the school with my sisters and me because the first return bus wasn't until the early afternoon, and there was too much for her to do around the property. She saw us off at the front gate, issuing instructions to the last moment.

'Listen to your sisters. Do what you're told. Don't act at school like you do here. Your play lunch is in your bag. So is your lunch. Wait for your sisters at the gate. Go, you'll be late.'

It had rained overnight, so the road and sidings were wet, muddy and slippery. Even if we had a car, it would probably have gotten bogged. There were only three houses on our street so the council did bugger all to the road. *What was the point?* they reckoned. They hadn't even run power or phone lines to our house, and our water came straight from our channel into water tanks.

We slipped and slid our way to the bus stop, passing tethered cows, grazing Clydesdales, tiny wagtails bathing in puddles, and vines and olive trees dripping with raindrops. The serenity was shattered, as my sleep had been, by Marlene's voice. 'I can hear the bus coming,' she yelled. 'Quick! Run!'

The bus was early. I found out later that when it rained, the bus was usually early because some of the kids couldn't make it due to the mud, and so it didn't have to stop so often.

'Quick! Run!' Marlene said again.

FIRST DAY OF SCHOOL

We sprinted through the mud, my sisters faster than me. 'Wait for me,' I screamed. Surely I wasn't going to miss the bus on my first day of school.

Pat, my other sister, stopped running and turned back for me. 'Don't worry,' she said. 'The bus driver has seen us.' She grabbed my hand and we ran together, her half-dragging me.

I climbed into the bus and looked down the aisle. The bus was packed with kids. I didn't know there were so many kids in the neighbourhood. There was no chance of getting a seat, it was standing room only.

'Down the back,' the driver yelled. 'Plenty of room today.'

I realised Pat was still holding my hand. I yanked it away. I didn't want anyone seeing me holding a girl's hand, let alone my sister's.

Far from getting nervous the closer we got to school, the more excited I got. The kids were all talking at once, louder and louder to be heard above each other. It was so animated. Then the bus flew through a huge puddle and water sprayed onto the windows, causing shrieks from the kids, and the driver to grip the wheel tight to keep control. I had never had so much fun.

We pulled up outside a school. 'Is this where we get off, sis?' I asked.

'No, not yet. This isn't our school. It's not far though.'

We squashed up as some of the kids got off the bus, then we were off again. This time we hit bitumen, so the bus sped up.

'Are we nearly there?'

'NO! Not yet!' My sister was getting annoyed with me.

We pulled up again. 'Is this it?'

'NO! Next stop.'

'It's such a long way,' I sighed.

There was no reaction.

I got a window seat for the final leg of the trip but had barely pressed my nose against the window when the bus started slowing down again.

'Surely ...' I started.

'Yes, we're there.'

As we got off the bus, on the corner of Deakin and Thirteenth Street, I couldn't help thinking it was a funny sight. All the boys dressed exactly like me, and all the girls dressed like my sisters.

'Come on, let's run,' I told my sisters.

One of them grabbed my arm. 'No,' she said. 'We can't run. We're not allowed. Ladies don't run.' I could hear the mockery in her tone.

So, we walked. It took so long.

As we got close to the school, I saw four nuns walking in formation. I had never seen nuns. They looked like something from another world, what with their long black dresses to the ground, covered foreheads, black veils with only their eyes, noses and mouths visible, and shiny black shoes. My goodness, they didn't have hands. Oh, yes, on closer look I realised their hands were tucked into their sleeves.

I felt another tug on my arm. 'Stop staring at the nuns,' Marlene whispered. 'Here's the school. I'll show you where your room is.'

We had to walk down a lane to get to the primary school. Towards the end of the lane, the school sprung into view: an old building constructed of galvanised iron and weatherboard. There was no grass in the playground, just gravel, though a row of peppercorn trees provided a small degree of nature.

The school was not the only building. Indeed, it was almost dwarfed by the church behind it, though if you entered from Eleventh Street, the main entrance, the school was behind the church. As I was to learn, nothing was more important than the church, especially not schoolchildren.

Marlene left me outside a room with my final instructions. 'Okay, John. This is your classroom. When the bell rings, you line up here. And when school is finished, you wait for me by the gate we came in, okay? Don't leave the gate until I come for you.'

And then she was off to the college building where all the big kids were.

I suddenly felt overwhelmed. There were kids running, playing, some holding their mum's hand. And nuns everywhere. I wandered away from the room to take it all in.

FIRST DAY OF SCHOOL

A bell rang and I looked across to see a nun strutting around the yard, swinging a bell above her head. A slight breeze meant her veil flowed behind her. It was quite a sight. I must have been staring for too long because she started striding towards me, and I realised the other kids had all raced to their rooms. I took off towards the room my sister had shown me.

As I got there, a nun standing at the doorway was ordering the kids to stand in a straight line with their mother beside them. Some of them were crying, which I thought was weird, particularly as they had their mum with them. I thought how nice it would have been to have my mum or dad there on my first day at school.

As the mothers left, the nun walked up and down the line of children, ordering the kids to line up straight, and using a strap to slap the legs of any kid not directly behind the one in front. I got a slap, which took me by surprise, but I didn't start crying, like many of the others who got the same treatment. Once the nun was satisfied, she marched us into class.

The classroom was much larger than I had imagined, and one of the walls held a huge blackboard, which the nun stood in front of. 'Pick a seat,' she told us, 'and sit down. Quietly!'

As soon as we had done so, she introduced herself as Sister Anthony. She looked ancient and I later found out that not only had she taught my sisters, but she was a young teacher there when my dad was working as a gardener at the school in his youth.

Sister Anthony started teaching us a prayer about some lady called Mary. It wasn't what I had expected to be learning at school. Her eyesight wasn't the best anymore, as she couldn't see past the students in the front three rows. Beyond them, she had to walk down the aisle between the seats to see who was there.

When the playtime bell rang, I ran outside with some of my classmates, and we walked around surveying the scene. The most popular game seemed to be marbles, with kids crouched around a crudely drawn circle flicking marbles from the edge of the circle, trying to hit the ones in the middle. I made a mental note to get myself some marbles.

The bell rang again way too quickly, and we were ushered back into the classroom to learn and recite more prayers. Only after lunch did we do anything resembling what I had expected to learn, spending the afternoon going over the ABCs.

By the time the final bell went, I had had enough. I was ready to go home. I waited at the gate as I had been told, and scanned the girls walking past to try to spot my sisters. Finally, they came. They were with some other girls, and when they collected me, they kept me slightly away from their friends, no doubt not wanting to be seen with me.

We walked back to the bus stop, and this time I got a seat for the whole trip. I must have been exhausted because I slept the whole way, having to be woken when we came to our stop.

*

That was my first day at school; for the first few years it was a fairly typical experience. As I got older, the discipline from the nuns became harsher. The whacks from the leather straps got harder. I once saw a nun grab a thin branch from a peppercorn tree and thwack a kid's legs while shouting, 'Pull your socks down.' After he did so, she thwacked him again, this time ordering, 'Pull your socks up.'

The only time I got into big trouble was when three other boys and I, standing at the trough in the toilet, tried to pee over the wall. It was something we did often, and it wasn't that hard because the wall was fairly low. Only on this occasion, as our wee disappeared over the wall, we heard a scream.

'You boys come out here now!'

Before we even got to the door, a nun was barging her way in, her strap raised in her wet hand. She whacked each of us as she ordered us back to class. She wasn't happy. No sense of humour.

FIRST DAY OF SCHOOL

With my dog Whitey (at three).

On the block at five – happy days.

Left to right: Marlene, Dad (Jack), Mum (Amy), me (at three) and Pat.

CHAPTER TWO

THE FIRES OF HELL

In 1954, when I was six and in grade two, they built us a new primary school, just 400 yards or so from the old tin sheds we had inhabited. We watched it being built from the ground up, our spirits and hopes high for a future of learning, caring and compassion. At the very least, we would be more comfortable, as the old school was so hot in the summer and icy cold in the winter. How on earth the nuns survived the 40°C+ temperatures covered in their black habits was beyond me. What I didn't know then was that I would gladly have traded the comforts of the new for the discomfort of the old in a flash. Even at the height of summer, it never got as bad as the fires of hell that awaited me.

When it was time to move into the newly built school, we gathered all our books, bags and everything else we could carry as we trudged down the road like worker ants. Before we left, one of my mates held up a leather strap he had found. 'What should I do with this?' he asked.

I looked around and pointed to a hole in a wall, of which there were many. 'Put it in there,' I said. 'There'll be one less strap for the nuns.'

The impetus behind the construction of a new school was the post-war influx of immigrants to Mildura (and indeed, Australia as a whole). The Snowy Mountains Scheme attracted many of them, but once here, the familiarity of farm work, particularly fruit growing and picking, saw some make their way to Mildura. Many of these were Italian Catholics and our church didn't want to miss out on the money and impressionable young minds on offer. Even in the new school they packed the kids in, as many as eighty in a single classroom. Learning was difficult and individual attention from teachers impossible to receive. So, any child who was a slow learner – and remember, many of the children could not speak English – had no chance.

It's fair to say there was nowhere to hide in school. If parents were behind in paying their school fees, they not only got a reminder, their children were also called out in front of class and paraded. Slow payers weren't the only ones embarrassed in this way. Every Monday, children were asked to raise their hands if they had not gone to church with their family on the Sunday prior. As a rule, our family did go to church – but when we didn't, because the road was too boggy or we were busy picking fruit, I kept my hand down. I knew it was a sin to lie but even worse was staying in at lunchtime reading our catechisms book, which was what those who'd missed church had to do. And I knew I wasn't the only one lying because on the occasions we did go to church, led by Mum who had strong Catholic beliefs, I did not see many of my classmates there.

When I hit grade three, it was time for my first Holy Communion and to start confessions. It was heavy duty religious studies in the lead-up to Communion Day, including several masses a week, which I didn't mind because it got me out of schoolwork.

It was during this time that I had my first experience with having the fire of hell put into me by a religious figure. Not physically – that was to come – but psychologically.

One Monday morning, we sat in class chattering about what we had done on the weekend when a nun walked into the room. We immediately stood, as we had been taught to do.

'Good morning children.'

'Gooood mooorning sister,' the chorus rang out.

She then explained that we were going to spend the morning practicing the rituals for the confessional, and after lunch, we were going to walk to the church for our first confessions. She emphasised the importance of the process. 'You have to confess your sins before your first Holy Communion. You can't have the blood of Christ with sins that you have committed. Your soul must be pure. God knows when you have sinned. You have a black mark on your soul, and he can see. If you have communion with a mark on your soul, you will burn in hell.'

To make sure we understood what a sin was, she wrote a list of sins on the blackboard.

- ◊   Being disobedient to nuns.
- ◊   Being disobedient to priests.
- ◊   Being disobedient to your parents.
- ◊   Being disobedient to any elders.
- ◊   Blaspheming.
- ◊   Not going to mass.
- ◊   Lying to a priest.

And on and on and on until the blackboard was chockablock of sins. Then she took us through the Ten Commandments so many times I could have recited them in my sleep.

After that, she ordered us to get out our exercise books and copy ten times what we had to say when we got into the confessional: *Bless me father for I have sinned. This is my first confession.*

As I wrote that line, over and over, I began thinking about the sins I was going to confess. I struggled for a while but then remembered – the leather strap. Thou shalt not steal. I looked over at my mate who had done the deed with me, and he must have been thinking the same as me because he gave me a knowing look. But then it wasn't really stealing, was it? We just hid it. And they just haven't found it, or maybe they have. Either way, forget about that one.

My next thought was to just make one up, but then I remembered, lying is a sin. How about swearing? Yes, I'll tell him I swore. No, he might ask me what I said and the only swear words I knew were those that dad used at home, and I don't want to repeat them. Hell! What was I going to say? That's it! Hell, that's blaspheming, twice now.

I wrote down blaspheming ten times in my book. I had my sin. I was ready to go. Then one of the girls raised her hand and asked a question. 'Sister, may I ask, what if you have no sins? What do you say then?'

'Well, my dear, just say you have no sins, and the priest will give you a blessing.'

Damn, that's the way to go, I thought.

That lunchtime was unlike any other. We didn't play football. We didn't run around. Everyone was so nervous. I started remembering what we'd been told about blaspheming, lying, not going to church – all the sins. The same phrases again and again:

Burn in hell.

Fire and brimstone.

Black spots on our souls.

I was overthinking everything. Saying hell wasn't really blaspheming because hell was the devil's domain. So, if I said I'd been blaspheming I'd really be lying – and that was a sin for which I could burn in hell. By the time the bell rang, I was in quite a state. And I wasn't the only one. As we walked to the church, one of the girls, Anna, burst out crying. I can still visualise that poor girl today. What was going through her mind? The doom? The gloom? The fires of hell? Such concepts and images to inflict on six-year-old children. Children's minds are like sponges. They learn what they live. I guess the Church knew that better than anyone.

And it's not just the ideas that are frightening. Churches are intimidating places and the Sacred Heart Church on Eleventh Street was no exception. Sturdy red brick with an apex pointing the way to heaven. The huge door was perhaps deliberately designed to put the fear of God into children as they huddled through, their chattering making way for silence. I walked in with a sense of awe, terror and wonderment. It wouldn't be long before the awe and wonderment disappeared, and terror was joined by fear.

Inside the church, it was eerie. Quiet at first, then a constant refrain of the sounds of confessional. Footsteps as we all wriggled down the aisles and sat down; the creaking of the seats as each kid got up to go to the confessional box; the door shutting quietly behind them; footsteps down the stairs as they left; the creaking of the kneeling plank as they knelt to recite their penance; jingling of the rosary beads that hung from the nuns' belt, nearly to the floor; shuffling as the nuns, vigilant to the last, ensured all went to plan.

I felt a touch on my shoulder. I looked up and a nun nodded at me. My turn. I stood, my stomach squirming, and slowly walked towards the confessional box. As I closed the door behind me, all light vanished. I blinked to orientate myself. Finally, I had adjusted so there was enough light to see where I was to kneel. In position, I looked to the tiny window where there was a silhouette of a face, hidden behind a drape.

My fear was intense. I wanted to run, to be sick, to be anywhere but there. My thoughts were shattered by a voice muttering something in Latin and then, 'Bless you my child, what are your sins?'

This was it. My time, my turn. I went blank. 'Ahhh … bless us Father, I did sin! Ahhh … no … ahhh …'

'Tell me your sins, my child.'

'I told a lie.'

'Is that all?'

'Yes, Father.'

More Latin and then, 'Say three Hail Marys for your penance, my child.' I stayed on my knees, expecting more, but then the priest said, 'You can go now, my son.'

'Thank you, Father.'

Back in the light, I found a seat to say my penance, and wondered how many it would have been if I had sworn. I reckoned my dad would have been here for a while.

It took time to get eighty children through their first confessional, but finally we were all done. Anna still had tears on her cheeks and a look of intense hurt and sadness.

Getting off the school bus in our street that afternoon, I was in another world. My sisters hurried ahead as my mind processed what we had just done, and what it meant – or what we had been taught it meant.

So many jumbled thoughts:

Do I still have black spots on my soul?

Am I going to burn in hell?

Is God watching me?

Can he see the spots?

Are the spots going to kill me?

What do I do about my first Holy Communion if I have spots on my soul?

Where is my soul?

Maybe Mum knows. She's old and wise. And if she doesn't, Dad will. He's always reading books.

As I got home, my dog, Whitey (because he was white), ran out to meet me as he always did. He ran around me in circles, then jumped up and licked me. It was always a warm welcome. But on this day, I had other things on my mind.

Walking into the house, I couldn't see Mum. Pat told me she was up on the block.

I walked through the vines and when I saw her, a few rows from me, I yelled, 'Mum, I'm home.'

She just walked away from me.

'HEY MUM,' I yelled again, in case she hadn't heard me. 'Mum, stop.'

She turned and asked impatiently, 'What do you want?'

'I have to tell you about school.'

'Not now. Your father is drinking with the neighbours and I have to get tea ready.'

We had tea that night in silence. Dad hadn't come home, which was not the first time, and no-one was talking because Mum was in a bad mood. All I wanted to do was tell them about my day and ask where the soul was, but I wasn't game.

We were sent to bed early, which suited me fine, as I was exhausted. Just as I was dropping off to sleep, I heard a commotion in the kitchen. It was Mum and Dad arguing, then a door slammed and Mum screamed, 'Jack, where are you going?' There was silence, followed by the sound of my mother talking to my sisters, and then my door opening and Mum telling me to get up and into the car.

Although Dad had gone, Mum knew he'd be back with a few more beers under his belt. He didn't drink every day, but when he did, he binged. Looking back, I suspect he suffered from depression brought on by the pressures of bills and repayments on the property. But he was a hard worker; we never did without. Those days were tough.

Mum drove down the road, then pulled up and parked in a siding. We slept that night in the car, my sisters in the back seat with Mum and me in the front. It wasn't the first time Mum had to deal with this. Dad didn't drink that often, but when he did, he made a good job of it. Still, it didn't make a lot of sense, the four of us sleeping in the car while Dad had the whole house to sleep off the booze.

I was woken by the car starting up. A tinge of sun filtered through the leaves of the trees we were parked under. A farmer was dragging her cow by a chain, moving it to a better grazing spot. Another farmer, with rubber boots, was checking the irrigation under his vines. Outside it was business as usual; in the back seat, my sisters were stretching and yawning.

Nothing was said on the way home, until we pulled into the driveway and Mum told us to pack for school while she got our lunches ready. We'd have to grab something for breakfast at school.

I arrived at school exhausted but there was no time for rest.

'Catechisms out, children,' came the cry from the nun only a moment after our bums had hit our chairs. 'Your Holy Communion is in a few days,' she went on, 'so I hope you are keeping your souls pure. If you don't, you need to tell me straight away so you can go to confession again the day before your communion. Remember, if you have a mark on your soul, God will see it and if you go to communion with a marked soul, you will burn in hell.'

From then until the day of communion, we did nothing in class except study the catechisms and the process for taking communion correctly. As we did, the nun walked up and down the aisle, face stern, tapping a leather strap against her side, her rosary beads jingling from her belt. At one point a child at the back of the classroom talked out of turn and the nun flew down the aisle, whacking him hard across the shoulder. It was not only a punishment for the boy, but also a warning to everyone else to keep their minds on their work.

THE FIRES OF HELL

Mum was excited that my first Holy Communion was approaching. She laid out my best clothes days in advance. She wouldn't have missed it for the world. Dad, though, was a different matter.

'Are you coming to my communion?' I asked him one evening.

'Nope,' was the immediate reply.

That wasn't a surprise to me. A disappointment, yes, but not a surprise. He never went to mass, even though he had been raised a Catholic. Mum had grown up in the Church of England but converted when she married Dad. She went to mass every Sunday unless it was impossible to get there.

After a week of intense religious learnings in the classroom, the big day arrived. My first Holy Communion. We usually went to the 7.00 am mass but this week we were going to the 8.30 mass, which meant a bit of a sleep-in. Even so, the household was frantic, with my sisters getting ready for the mass and Mum making some last-minute alterations to a dress she had made for herself for the occasion.

I played outside with Whitey until the last possible moment, with Mum yelling at me to get ready or we'd be late. I couldn't shake the thought of where my soul was and what marks it might have on it. I was worried I hadn't told the priest enough – that I might have blasphemed or not obeyed my parents and not confessed those sins. Would God strike me down for having spots on my soul? So many thoughts running through my mind.

I dressed in the shirt, jacket and tie that had been laid out for me. But the pants were short. I told mum that long pants would be better but she responded, 'Little boys don't wear long pants.'

With long grey socks up to my knees, I thought I looked a little ridiculous but Mum wouldn't change her mind.

Sitting in the back of the car, I asked Pat, 'Where's my soul?'

'It's all over you,' she said.

'All over? How can that be?'

'Your soul is you, it's who you are, it's the part that God watches.'

'So, if you have spots on your soul, the spots are all over me?'

'Yes, that's right. Why?'

'I was just wondering.'

Turning the corner near the church, I couldn't believe how many people were there. Two or three times more than for normal mass. I guess it made sense. There were eighty children from my class all doing their communion, with parents, grandparents and siblings there to share the experience. Inside the church, a nun was directing the kids to the front of the church. I turned and waved at my mum and sisters, who found seats in the body of the church.

The church was a hive of activity. Women volunteers buzzed around the altar, setting up flowers for the Lord, continually bowing their heads and kneeling in respect. A priest also fiddled around with preparing the altar. Nuns paced up and down and huddled in corners, having conferences.

Soon, the start of a hymn could be heard, very softly, and then louder as the head priest emerged, clad in long robes with gold edges and the symbol of the cross, and headgear as elaborate as a bishop's.

He took off his headgear and addressed the congregation, telling them that the mass would be longer than usual because of the children taking their first Holy Communion. Nerves kicked in at that point, though I tried to resist fidgeting. We had been given strict instructions to sit still, with our hands folded in our laps. The nuns watched us like hawks.

Finally, it was time for our communion. The kids closest to the front got up and inched forward. I watched them, my stomach heaving with nerves. Nuns helped control the lines up and then back. All I could think was, am I going to be struck down if I've got marks on my soul?

It was my turn. I stood, wobbling a little as my legs were like jelly. I concentrated hard and walked to the front to receive the sacraments. I kneeled alongside a line of other children and the priest walked past, putting the bread on our tongues. As he gave me mine, he touched my head with his hand, then moved on. And that was it, except for the certificate we were handed as a commemoration of our first Holy Communion.

On the way back to my seat, I felt the bread stick to the roof of my mouth, but I put up with it. The nuns had told us not to chew the sacrament because it would bleed and run from our mouth, and that it would be Christ's blood. So, I resisted touching it and felt it gradually dissolving in my mouth.

After what seemed an eternity, it was all over, and we were hustled out a side door where the Reverend Mother addressed us. 'I'm very pleased with you all today,' she said. 'Everything went very well. When you go home, I want you to reflect on this day and thank God for the rest of the day. Now go quietly back to your parents and pray to Jesus to keep your soul pure.'

And that was my Holy Communion day.

The priest who had conducted the communion was Father John Day, and he was new to the parish. After one Sunday mass, as we sat as a family eating a breakfast of sausages and eggs, Mum told Dad that Father Day had given a very strong sermon that day about how he did not like what was happening in the town, and that the church had to be made bigger and stronger. The means for that, of course, came in the mighty dollar, or pound in those days. He was going to hand out envelopes with a family's name on each – money was to be placed inside the envelope as a donation.

Dad hit the roof. He told Mum that there wasn't enough money in the town for people to give more but Mum insisted she would do her best to find a way. They argued all day about it, but I'm sure Mum managed to slip extra money onto the plate from then on, as did many families who could least afford it.

Years later, in his statement to the Royal Commission into Institutional Responses to Child Sex Abuse, Father Gerald Baldock made reference to Father Day's wealth and love of money. In part, his statement reads:

> I remember the first time I ever heard a story about Monsignor DAY. It was when I was in about fourth year in the seminary (around 1967 or 1968). Someone told me a joke that the Anglican priest came to Monsignor DAY and said, 'Look, you seem to be quite wealthy, you know. What's the secret?' And Monsignor DAY said, 'Well, on Sunday, I get

all the collections and I put them in a great big basket and throw them all up in the air and what stays up there, that's God's, and what comes down is mine.'

Looking now at the extensions and renovations of the Sacred Heart Church, and the acquisition of property around it, a shit load of it must have come down.

Standing in front of the chook house – all dressed up for Holy Communion certificate.

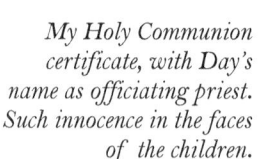

My Holy Communion certificate, with Day's name as officiating priest. Such innocence in the faces of the children.

CHAPTER THREE

SISTER BARNARD

At the end of grade three, I was told that I was going to have to repeat the year. I was younger than most of my classmates, and the intensive learning for Holy Communion had put me behind where I should have been. I guess my classmates had managed that better than me. Still, I was happy with the decision, particularly as my best friend, on the next block to ours, would now only be one grade behind me. Mum and Dad also thought it was probably for the best.

It was much easier for me the second time around, particularly as I didn't have to repeat all the lessons on the catechisms and confession. I had plenty of time on my hands, and also caught up a bit on the non-religious subjects.

My school years, to that point, were the happiest of my life – and unfortunately would remain so for the rest of my life. The discipline and nuns aside, school wasn't too bad. And weekends were spent on the fruit block with Dad. He taught me how to drive the tractor and I would furrow the ground between the rows of vines, getting it ready for the irrigation.

In the evenings, when the work was done, we would go shooting for rabbits and hares, not primarily for their meat (hares are almost inedible anyway), but because they would chew through the young vines. Of course, we did eat the rabbits, but I sold the hares for two shillings each to an old man who lived nearby. He would hang the hares in a tree for a couple of days, then bury them for another two days. After digging them up, he would skin, gut and bake them. It was known as jug hare. According to Dad, you had to add a hell of a lot of other stuff to it to make it taste any good.

About the only thing I wasn't looking forward to that year was Sister Barnard. Sister Barnard was hard to ignore. For one thing, she ran everywhere. Sometimes it was because she was running late but often it was just the way she was. But the main reason was her delight in humiliating children. Unfortunately, she was my class teacher that year.

Sister Barnard had one hell of a reputation, enhanced by an incident early one year when, perhaps to send a warning, she called a boy to the front of assembly in front of the entire school. She yelled at him, then gave him six hard smacks with an open hand across his face and told him to sit down again. He turned on his heels, an action that displeased Sister Barnard. She called him back and gave him a further six whacks across the face.

'Don't you ever walk away from me like that again,' she told him.

In the classroom, students lived in fear of Sister Barnard, cowering as she ran up and down the aisles, her eyes darting to make sure work was being done. Anyone who lifted their head got the strap across their hands or a ruler across their fingers for their troubles. One time, she broke a boy's finger, which resulted in complaints from his parents and, ultimately, a cover-up by the nuns and the Church. Cover-ups come naturally to the Church.

One Monday, towards the end of grade four, I was walking down the church aisle before the start of morning mass and confessional when Sister Barnard stopped me and gestured for me to sit beside her, which I did. A little later, she flicked me with her strap and nodded towards the confessional box. Clearly it was my turn.

Once I had knelt, the priest began speaking and I realised it was Father Day. I confessed and he told me to repent my sins, but then he asked me if there was anything else I should tell him. There was nothing I could think of, but he persisted. Finally, he let me go, but I left hoping I didn't have to confess to him again.

Later that day, in church again, Father Day gave us a sermon about the fires of hell and the importance of children keeping their souls pure at communion. Then we lined up as usual to accept the sacrament. Father Day walked along the line, giving the bread to every child, but when he came to me, he stopped a little bit longer than he had with the others, and touched my head, which he hadn't with anyone else. The only thing I could think of was that he hadn't believed my confession, or that he possessed superpowers and knew I had forgotten something. But what?

*

The next day, in class, I was mucking around with the boy sitting next to me; we were hitting each other on the legs. The other boy gave a sharp yelp and Sister Barnard swirled around to see me pulling my hand back.

'Mr Fitzgibbon, you come up here now,' she shrieked. 'Sit on the platform and I'll deal with you later.'

As it was approaching lunchtime, I thought my punishment may be to stay in over lunch – not too bad. When the bell went, Sister Barnard seemed preoccupied with packing up and putting stuff in her bag. I got up as unobtrusively as I could and moved to the door, thinking she may not notice or may have forgotten about me. No such luck.

'Don't you move. Stay there,' she yelled, almost exactly the way Dad shouted at Whitey.

Things then went from bad to worse. She grabbed my ear and pulled me out of the classroom, all the while clutching her bag with her other hand. She was walking so fast, I almost had to run to keep up, and not to trip over. Obviously, this was in full view of the students having lunch and playing.

I realised she was taking me to the church. As we got close, I saw Father Day sitting on a chair on the veranda of the presbytery, where the priest lived. Sister Barnard made a beeline for him, and he looked up as we neared.

'Excuse me Father,' she said. 'This boy has been naughty. I would like you to deal with him.'

'Leave him with me,' he said. 'I'll deal with him.'

She not only left me with Father Day, but also with a red, sore ear. I stood in front of Father Day, almost peeing myself in fear.

'What do you have to say for yourself, young man?' he said, gazing down at me.

I was trembling. 'I'm sorry, Father,'

'Well, what are you going to say at your next confession?'

'I'm sorry I've been bad in class.'

That seemed to make him happy, but he added, 'You don't want me to tell your parents, do you?'

'No Father, please no.'

And he told me to run along.

I didn't feel like facing everyone in the playground, so as I passed the peppercorn trees between the church and the school, I climbed one of them as high as I could and perched on a branch. I wondered why I'd been singled out to see Father Day. It had been so humiliating being dragged past everyone. Oh, to be a bird and able to fly from that tree. When the bell went, I stayed put. After all, Sister Barnard would have had no idea how long Father Day had kept me for. I was up there for an hour.

The following week, as we were led to the church for confession, I had just one thing on my mind – to avoid the box with Father Day in it. Inside the entrance, Sister Barnard was telling the children where to sit. As I got to her, she pushed me into a seat at the back and on the right hand side of the aisle.

I peered to the front where the four confessional boxes stood. I didn't take my eyes off them. When the priests walked in, I hoped with all my might that Father Day would take a box on the left-hand side. No such luck. He walked towards a box on my side, turned, spotted me, and seemed to nod and wink my way. It was almost as if it was pre-arranged.

Then came the poke from Sister Barnard, disturbing my daydream about being home instead of in church. It was my turn. The confession box seemed darker than usual, and I almost missed the board as I knelt. I shuffled forward as Father Day gave the Latin preamble and then it was my turn.

'Bless me Father for I have sinned, it has been five days since my last confession.'

'Yes, my son. What are your sins?'

'I was bad in school, Father, and I …'

He cut me short. 'What did you do?' he asked.

'I was messing around with another boy and I punched him. Just messing around, Father.'

'Punching someone is not messing around, my son. So, what other sins are on your soul?'

I paused, then, 'I swore in the school ground.'

'You are at a Catholic school. We don't stand for that sort of thing.'

'Yes Father.'

'Any other sins on your soul, my son?'

'No Father.'

He told me that my sins were serious and that my penance for my sins was six Our Fathers and six Hail Marys. I went to stand but he added, 'I want to see you soon about your punching in class.'

I thought that was unusual but said, 'Yes Father.'

As I knelt to say my penance, I could feel Sister Barnard's steely eyes on me. I stayed there until I sensed she was busy seeing other children out, then as quietly as I could, I shuffled to the end of the row and headed down the aisle. Suddenly, a hand gripped my arm and yanked me into a seat. A couple of the schoolgirls noticed and started giggling. They left, followed by others, until Sister Barnard and I were the only ones left sitting in the body of the church.

I watched as three of the priests walked out of the church together, but Father Day was not one of them. The door of the confessional box I'd been in opened, and there he was.

As he walked towards us, he thanked Sister Barnard and told me I had to have a lesson about my behaviour. He put his hand on my back and led the way through a side door, while Sister Barnard walked out the front, her hands buried in her sleeves.

From the side door of the church, Father Day hustled me towards the presbytery. He kept his hand in contact with my back as we stepped up to the veranda. He then reached ahead of me to open the door. Inside, he offered me a lemonade. 'No thank you Father,' I said. But he insisted.

He showed me into a semi-dark room and went to fetch the lemonade. There was a couch on one side of the room, and a small table in the centre, with books stacked high. On the other side, against the wall, were two armchairs side-by-side, under a picture of The Last Supper. I was busting for a pee and started crossing my legs to ease the pressure on my bladder, when Father Day walked back in. He pushed the books to one side and placed the glass of lemonade on the table.

'May I use the toilet please Father,' I squirmed.

He thought for a moment then told me that the toilet was on the other side of the meeting room, and that a meeting was in progress. 'We can't disturb the meeting,' he said, 'but wait a moment, I'll fetch a bucket for you.'

I stood there pressing my legs together. He returned and handed me a bucket. I took it and looked around. I did not want to pee in front of him.

'Come on,' he said. 'We have the same thing. Would you like me to help you?'

'I'm okay thanks, Father.'

I took the bucket to the corner and placed it on the floor but before I could undo my buttons, I started to wet myself. I tried to direct some of the pee into the bucket, but it was too late. It went down my legs and started to form a puddle on the floor.

'Oh dear, you really did need to go, didn't you Johnny?' Father Day said. 'I'll get a towel. You take your pants off and I'll wipe you down.'

I panicked at the thought. 'It's okay, Father. By the time I get back to school it will be dry.'

He would have nothing of it. He insisted I remove my pants and reminded me we had not yet talked about my so-called misbehaviour.

Father Day started to undo my pants. Then he got me to lie on the couch so he could pull them off. He tried to pull my underpants off with them but I grabbed the waistband tight.

'Come on, let go,' he said. 'You can't have wet undies on.'

So the undies came off as well.

While he found a place to hang my clothes, I pulled the bottom of my shirt down as far as I could, to cover myself.

He joined me on the couch and put his arm around me. 'Now let's talk about you punching other boys. I think I should tell your parents.'

'No, Father.'

'I think I should.'

As he spoke, he started wiping my legs with the towel, up to my groin, around my private parts, then back down my legs.

'That feels good, doesn't it?' he said. 'Now, just relax. I won't hurt you and I won't tell your parents if you're a good boy. Lay back, let go of your shirt. It's okay. You're a very special boy, you know that? Now roll onto your side and I'll wipe the back of your legs.'

He wiped the towel over my bum and between my legs. He then grabbed hold of my penis and started to rub it. I felt my stomach heave.

'That feels good, doesn't it Johnny? I've got the same but mine's bigger. Would you like to look at it? Here, give me your hand.'

He rolled me over. He had his pants down and his large penis was sticking out, straight. He put my hand on it and then placed his hard over mine, squeezing it slightly. Then he started moving our hands up and down along his penis.

'Yours will be big like this when you're older, and it will get hard like this. But remember, this is our secret, okay?'

The pain in my stomach became intense and I wanted to cry, but didn't dare. He rolled me onto my stomach and put his knees on each side of me. I felt the head of his penis between the cheeks of my bum, then penetrating, slowly at first, then harder, going back and forth and back and forth, hurting like hell, until something warm and wet ran between my legs. I didn't understand what was happening to me, why he was doing this, and what the wetness was between my legs. He wiped the cheeks of my bum and between my legs again.

'You're very special, Johnny,' he said, 'and this is our secret, okay? If you tell anyone, I'll tell your parents that you've been bad.

They won't believe you about today, anyway. Now get dressed, your clothes should be dry. I'll fetch something special for you.'

Father Day left the room and I couldn't get my clothes on quick enough. My legs felt sticky, my pants were still wet, and my stomach ached, but I was just focussed on getting out of there. He returned with some chocolate, reminded me that this was a secret and sent me on my way.

Once outside, I started to run, but I stopped at the peppercorn tree I had climbed before. It was only about fifty metres from the presbytery but its many branches and generous foliage ensured noone could see me in there, not even Day. I scaled the branches like a possum, hurtling from one to another until I was embedded in the middle. There, I settled, my heart thumping. A feeling of shame overwhelmed me and I wept solidly for an hour or so. I could not make sense of what had happened. Again, I wished I could fly away. Or hide in the peppercorn tree forever. Only here was I safe.

Eventually, I climbed down and went back to school. The kids were coming out of class for playtime. I grabbed my bag and ate my lunch. Back in the classroom, I could not concentrate. Whatever Father Day had put on my legs was sticking to my pants. My mind continued wandering.

Please God, whatever I have done, forgive me. Don't let Father Day do that to me again. I'll be real good, I promise. Can you hear me, God? I am so sorry.

My thoughts were shattered with a whack across my hands from Sister Barnard's strap. I pulled my hands away and put them under my desk.

'Put your hands back on the desk, Fitzgibbon,' she ordered. 'And why haven't you got any work done? There's not a single thing in your book. Why not?'

'I don't know, sister.'

'You don't know, sister? Well, you'd better know. You will with this.'

And she gave me six hard whacks across the back of my hands and for the rest of the day I had to do my schoolwork on the blackboard in front of the class.

Lying in my bed that night, I couldn't sleep. I felt the need to tell someone about what had happened. But who? I heard Dad making a cup of tea in the kitchen and went to him. He was sitting at the table reading.

'Dad,' I said.

He looked up. 'What?'

I stood there, as if frozen to the spot. What to do?

'It's okay,' I said finally, and went back to bed. I couldn't tell him. I couldn't tell anyone. Who would believe me over the word of a priest? No-one.

During the night, I had to go to the toilet. It was an outside toilet with a long drop, and we used newspaper as toilet paper. When I'd finished wiping, I noticed blood on the paper. No wonder it had hurt so much. I sat on the toilet and cried my eyes out. I slept little the rest of that night.

The next morning, I asked Mum if I could stay home from school because I didn't feel well. She just told me I looked alright and, besides, there would be no-one at home to look after me.

'I'll be okay by myself,' I insisted. But she gave me short thrift.

The only positive was that it was near the end of the school year and I'd be out of there for the summer.

At the last few assemblies, we were constantly reminded about the upcoming end-of-year exams, and that during the holidays we had to continue to go to mass and confession.

The exams lasted the best part of a week but I couldn't concentrate on them. I kept thinking about what Father Day had done to me, whether he would come for me again, and, if so, how I could possibly keep him away.

It was no surprise to me that I failed the exams. However, my school report indicated that I had worked well for most of the year, and that it was only towards the end that I lost focus. As a result, I would not have to repeat the year again. Mum, though, was far from happy with my report. She told me to knuckle down the next year, and bemoaned the fact I wasn't as smart as my sisters.

The Christmas holidays began and though I knew I would still see Father Day at church, dragged there because of Mum's devotion, I knew he wouldn't be able to get me back into the presbytery. I was safe for now.

Me, second from left at some sort of performance in the school playground. I still had an optimistic outlook on life here, but that feeling wasn't going to last much longer. John believes the woman circled is Judy, his friend and soulmate.

Me at eight on a tractor on the block.

My official school photo at age eleven. Believe me, that smile was well and truly forced.

Another photo at around the same time.

The presbytery today – little changed from when Day first led me in there.

CHAPTER FOUR

MY JOURNAL

It was Christmas Eve 1957. While Mum and my sisters were busy in the kitchen getting things ready for Christmas Day, Dad and I were catching chooks and chopping off their heads. They would take pride of place at our Christmas dinner. Dad didn't mind doing the chopping but said his gnarly farmer hands were no good for plucking. And gutting them made him squeamish. So, Mum did the plucking and the gutting.

I helped Dad hang the chooks on the clothesline, so that the blood would drain out. Then Dad told me to take some milk to the Italian neighbours and pick up some vegetables in return. When I got back, Dad was at his desk, writing notes into a thick, tattered book. I asked him what he was doing, and he told me he was jotting down what we needed for the upcoming harvest. Then he showed me the book.

'It's my journal,' he said. 'It's an account of what's happened over the years during harvests, with the pickers, when I've taken irrigation water, how much fruit I've grown … all sorts of things for the last 15 years.'

I was astounded. Such history. I asked him if he'd written when I was born, and he flicked through the book to 1948 and showed me. Wow. At that moment, I decided to keep a journal.

I rushed to my room and found an exercise book with nothing written in it. That would do. Next, I needed a hiding place for it. There was a hole in my wardrobe where it would fit. Perfect.

I now had a way to express my thoughts about what was happening in my life, at school and at home. Most importantly, I now had someone, or rather something, I could talk to about Father Day. I started immediately to write about Father Day and what he did. I wrote a poem and let my frustrations run from inside me onto the page. It helped me in a way nothing else had.

For children, Christmas Eve is a time for immense excitement and anticipation. Father Day had spoilt it for me because that evening, apart from writing about him and what he had done, I couldn't get out of my mind the fact that I would see him in the morning at mass.

That night I had a nightmare. I was trapped in a small, dark room, with the door locked. A sickly, sweet smell pervaded the space. There was just enough light to make out someone in black floating on the ceiling, waving for me to join them. Another identical figure appeared, also waving at me. They called for me and then descended, coming towards me. Then I woke. Or at least I think I did. There seemed to be someone in black standing at the end of my bed. I started sweating and shaking, and stayed as still as I could. Then I heard a noise somewhere in the house, and light seeped under my bedroom door. Someone was up. I got out of bed, turned on my light and opened my door. Someone had just been to the toilet. I went back to bed and lay there, my light still on. It stayed on for the rest of the night.

'Merry Christmas,' my mum yelled as she rose everyone up.

I hadn't been back to sleep and welcomed the comfort of Mum's greeting.

I got dressed and went into the kitchen. Everyone was swapping Christmas greetings. Then came the moment I was dreading.

'Come on kids,' Mum said, 'We don't want to be late for Christmas mass.'

*

Standing at the front of the church was a large man, almost as wide as he was tall. He was in a suit, inspecting everyone who arrived and handing out the envelopes for donations. I hadn't seen him before but found out later that he was a police officer, Jim Barritt, later to become a detective senior sergeant in Melbourne.

We usually sat towards the middle of the church but today there were so many people, the only available seats were near the front or the back. To my dismay, Mum walked to the front where we found seats only six rows in; way too close for my liking, considering that Father Day was giving the mass.

Being a Christmas mass, two priests were going to officiate. They walked in, one of them Father Day. Though I knew he'd be there, the sight of him caused my stomach pains to return. I just wanted him to disappear.

The mass seemed to go on forever, and when it came time for the sermon, Father Day walked up onto the pulpit, clutching a huge bible against his stomach. He began by reminding everyone about the envelopes they had, and the need for the extra money, stressing that despite the envelopes, normal donations to the plate were still expected.

Then he railed against what he saw happening in Mildura. He preached about the importance of virginity, celibacy, chastity and morality. He made mention of an article in a Mildura newspaper that had a photo of local girls parading in bikinis. He called it degrading, indecent and un-Christian. What about what he had done to me?

He went on to say that we would all pay for our sins on Judgement Day; that we would burn in hell. As he said it, he spotted me and his eyes stayed fixed on me for a while. I looked down, as if praying, but my eyes were filling with tears, and my stomach aching.

There were three priests giving communion, and when the time came, I was clever enough to position myself to miss him. However, he made sure he walked past and gave me a stern look.

I dawdled out of church a little after Mum, and when I got out, I was dismayed to see her talking to Father Day. Was he telling her I had been bad at school? Surely not. She stood speaking to him for ages, but walked to us with a smile, so he couldn't have told her.

It was during these holidays that I became a loner. Instead of playing with friends, I worked on the fruit block with Dad, driving the tractor and immersing myself in a world of make-believe. Sometimes I imagined I was a cowboy on a horse, at other times a racing car driver. Anything to avoid thoughts about Father Day.

One evening at dinner, I built up the courage to tell my parents that I didn't like my school and wanted to go to the state school nearby. Well, the way Mum reacted, you'd have through I'd chopped off the head of her prize-winning chook.

'State school?' she exclaimed. 'How could you even think of such a thing? You will be staying at the Sacred Heart School and that's that. You nearly failed last year. You'll get nowhere at a state school.'

I didn't raise it again.

*

Walking into the school grounds for the first day of grade four, I felt sick. I didn't want to play with my friends, I didn't want to go into class. I just didn't want to be there. I sat myself down on a log and looked into the distance.

When the bell rang, I slowly got up and moved over to where the other children were lining up for assembly. The nuns were also getting into place in front of their new classes. I feared the worst but couldn't see Sister Barnard anywhere. Whispers ran up and down the line. 'Where is she?' 'Where's Sister Barnard?' 'Don't know.' 'Have you seen her?' 'No.'

Word finally filtered back to us that Sister Barnard had moved to Melbourne, and I prayed that Father Day had gone as well, but it wasn't to be.

By now, the influx of immigrants had boosted numbers in our school to the point there were ninety children in my class. Most were Italian and could hardly speak English. It was quite a challenge for our teacher, Sister Angela, who was a hit from the start because she started the first class of the year by reading to us. She turned out to be one of the best teachers I had.

That night, in my bedroom, I opened my journal and wrote about my feelings in the form of a poem:

> Who would believe me? Are you a liar? Or are you crazy?
>
> There's no one I can tell!
>
> I feel my heart beating fast.
>
> Anxiety attacks, I am feeling ill.
>
> Black box I can't get out!
>
> Who can I see?
>
> Who can I tell?

The following day, as I walked into school, I saw three cars: a police car, a large blue Pontiac, and a plainer car. In the assembly area, Detective Jim Barritt stood with two uniformed police officers, talking to Father Day. It wasn't long before I found out what was going on. I poked my head into my classroom where students' desks had been upended, Sister Angela's desk had been smashed, and on the blackboard was scrawled: 'The nuns can get fucked', 'Father Day is a fucking shithead' and 'The Catholic Church is bullshit.'

A nun tapped me on the leg with her strap and told me to get back into the playground. She stayed near the door, so no one else could get a look. Even in the playground, there were further signs of vandalism, with ink poured over the concrete. It was some mess.

We were kept in the playground for an hour longer than usual, and then the uniformed police and Father Day left, with Father Day driving the Pontiac. I couldn't help wondering how he got the money for it.

We lined up for assembly and Detective Barritt stood next to the Reverend Mother. She grabbed the microphone and began proceedings.

'Last night we had a break-in,' she said. 'A lot of desks were tipped upside down in the grade four classroom and Detective Barritt here would like to know why. There are six students whose desks were untouched, and they are all boys. As I read the names of those boys out, I want them to come up here.'

I hadn't seen clearly enough whether my desk had been touched and I crossed my fingers it had been tipped over, but the third last name she called was mine. Six of us lined up in front of the school, as if we were suspects.

Detective Barritt led us into the Reverend Mother's office and made us stand in a line against the wall. 'This is how it works,' he said. 'I am going to ask each of you some questions. And even if you did not do anything, but know who did and don't tell me, you will be in as much trouble as the boy who did it. Do you understand?'

We nodded.

He asked what time we had left school the day before, where we were during the night and what time we had arrived at school that morning. No-one had been anywhere they shouldn't have been. Then he took us outside and got us to line up an arm's length from each other, positioned so he could see us from inside.

'I'm going to interview you all one at a time,' he said. 'I don't want any of you talking out here while I do so, RIGHT?'

Again, we just nodded.

I was the fourth in line, and so stood there while three others went in first. It was a horrifying experience as he was so menacing, towering above us at about six foot two.

'NEXT!' he shouted, and I realised it was my turn. He held the door open and as I passed him, he shut the door and ordered me to sit. I hadn't even put my bum on the seat when he started.

'Your name?'

'John.'

'FULL NAME.'

And so it went. Where I lived, where I was at certain times. Could my parents vouch for those times? Did I know who had vandalised the school? Could I guess who might have done it? Of course I said no.

I didn't tell Mum and Dad what had happened at school that day. I was afraid I'd be in trouble. After all, I was interviewed by a detective. I hoped that Barritt would not get in touch with my parents.

CHAPTER FIVE

RUNNING AWAY

There was a loud knock on the classroom door and Sister Angela went to open it. Standing there was a solidly built man wearing a suit. He showed her his wallet, then talked, while she just nodded. Finally, she turned back into the classroom, walked down the aisle, stopped at my desk and bent over to whisper, 'The man at the door is a detective and he's investigating the break-in. He wants you to go with him.' She reassured me that he was going to interview other boys as well, but I wasn't sure I believed her.

I expected to be taken to another school room but instead he led me to his car, opened the door, saw me in, and then started driving. I felt sick.

I gathered the courage to ask, 'Where are you taking me?'

'Not far,' was all he said.

I looked out the window. We drove along Twelfth Street, left into Langtree Parade, then left again into Eleventh Street. I realised we were going to the church. When he pulled up alongside the curb, I told him, 'I don't want to go in there.'

He grabbed my arm and told me Father Day wanted to talk about the break-in. I tried to pull away and started crying.

'I don't want to go in there,' I pleaded.

He just grabbed me tighter. At that point, Father Day came out; he told me to go inside and wait for him. As I started, I heard him thank the detective.

From inside, I could still hear snatches of conversation from outside. There was mention of money and Detective Barritt, then the detective left and I watched as Father Day approached the door. Seconds later we were alone inside.

'I haven't seen you for a while, have I Johnny?'

'No Father.'

He asked if I had anything to do with the break-in and told me my mother had told him I often wasn't at home. Of course I denied anything to do with the vandalism and explained that when I wasn't at home, I was on the fruit block with my dad. He persisted and I burst out crying, not so much from the questioning but anticipation of what might happen next. He put his arm around me and squeezed me so tight I could hardly breathe.

'Calm down,' he told me. 'Remember you're special, Johnny. Now, I think you were at school when it was broken into but if you're a good boy I won't say anything, and I'll keep the police away from you.'

I was too shocked and upset to say anything. And I knew what was going to happen next.

Father Day inched closer to me, increased his grip and kissed me on the top of my head. He then slithered a hand down to my crotch and started lightly squeezing my genitals. He pulled his penis out and started to play with it. He then let go and started to undress me. As he did, he reminded me of a few things.

'Now, remember our deal. You be a good boy and I won't tell on you. If I told the police and your parents about you, they would send you to a boys' home and you'd never see your family again. Would you like that?'

'No Father.'

'So, what are you going to do?'

'Be a good boy, Father.'

'Now give my dick a rub like I showed you. That's a good boy. That feels good.'

He had me believing I would be sent to a boys' home if I told anyone. He had the police on his side. He had nuns on his side. I was powerless.

As soon as I got home, I went straight to some dense bushland on our property and sat among the trees crying my eyes out. I prayed: *Please God, make Day go away. Do I deserve what he is doing to me? Can you help? I didn't do the things he said I did. Please help me.*

It would be better to be dead then this. Just show me what to do, give me a sign.

But there was no sign. No help. God wasn't listening to me. I yelled, 'You're not there, are you?' The scribble on the backboard was right, the Church is full of bullshit.

Weekends started taking on new meaning. They were time out from school and Father Day. But one weekend jolted me back to reality. I was in my bedroom writing in my journal about Father Day when I heard the phone ring. We hadn't had a phone for long, so when it rang, it was a novelty, and everyone wondered who it might be.

The call was from Marlene's boyfriend, Ted, asking her to go horse riding with him. She asked Mum and Dad if she could borrow the car, and they agreed. I then asked if I could tag along but Mum said 'No.' I pleaded but got nowhere. I kept at Mum and eventually she snapped, 'I said no and that's that. If you keep this up, we'll send you to boarding school. You've been behaving badly lately, so go to your room and don't come out until I tell you to come out.'

I couldn't believe it. This was what Father Day had threatened. What was happening? I went to my room and wrote in my journal:

> Dear journal, please tell me why people want to send me away I am not bad not real bad it's father Day he's bad not me or is he allowed to be bad because he's got god on his side and the police.
>
> I would like to run away where can I go if I do I promise I'll take you with me. I've got no one else to talk to but you, and I would like to go horse riding with my sister.

Then I had an idea. If I could sneak into the car without my sister knowing, I could get away from home. So, I packed a bag with my journal, pocketknife, two pencils, and a box of matches that I used at home to check for spiders when I went to the outside toilet.

As my sister was getting ready to leave, I snuck out of the house and climbed into the boot of the car. My parents' car was a Morris Standard Ten and the back seats folded down, so I had plenty of fresh air and could push the seat a bit to see outside. I made myself as comfortable as possible as I waited for my sister.

I felt movement and then the car started up. We probably only got as far as the end of the drive when I thought this might not be such a good idea. But it was too late. I then thought that if I got caught, I'd be sent to a boys' home, but the risk was worth it. I had to get away from Father Day any way I could.

I felt the car go across a bridge, then onto a dirt road. I wasn't exactly sure where we were but I didn't care. Finally, the car slowed down and stopped. The car door opened then was shut.

There was silence for a while. I wanted to know what was happening but wasn't game to move. Then I heard voices near the car. I expected to hear the doors open but they didn't. The voices got quieter and quieter as the people got further away, until I couldn't hear them at all.

I pushed the back seat forward and slowly raised my head to the window. I could see Marlene and Ted talking to another man. They had their backs to me, so I pushed the seat forward a bit more. I could see the bush outside; there were plenty of hiding places. I decided to make a dash for it.

As I started climbing over the back seat, Marlene turned around and looked towards the car. She said something that I couldn't hear but I could clearly read her lips. 'John. Oh no.' She ran to the car. 'What are you doing?' she screamed at me. 'What are Mum and Dad going to say?'

I didn't say anything but knew I was in trouble.

We drove to Ted's parents' house, so Marlene could call our parents. I didn't have to lie in the boot this time, but I had plenty of time to think of the trouble I was in. My parents weren't home. Of course they weren't. They were out looking for me. Calls were made to neighbours to alert my parents but most of the neighbours were out looking for me as well. Some were dragging local channels and dams with rakes, in case I had drowned. Finally, a neighbour was reached and the search was called off.

When I got home, Mum was in one hell of a mood. It wasn't just the upheaval I had caused. Dad was with some neighbours and was drinking. According to Mum, that was my fault as well.

I went to my room, unpacked my bag, and wrote in my journal:

> Showed his badge to take me away.
>
> Put you in a home. That's where you will go.
>
> You're a bad boy.
>
> I'll run away. But doesn't work.
>
> Undressing me again.
>
> Hands all over. Please stop.
>
> Got me where he wants me.
>
> Everyone is powerless against father Day.

*

My abuse from Father Day increased until he would regularly call me into the presbytery for just ten minutes, so no one would miss me or wonder where I was. He reinforced that this was all my fault and I started to believe him. I got further and further behind in my schoolwork but didn't care.

One saint's day, while we were being supervised from school to church for mass, I decided I was going to skip mass. I went to the toilet as everyone was lining up to go, and stayed there until I knew everyone would be in church. Then I ran down the lane, in the opposite direction to the church.

Where to go? I couldn't go home as Mum and Dad would be there. It was only 10 am, so I had a lot of time to fill until the end of school. If I wandered the street, someone would see me and maybe report me to the school, so I walked through paddocks to the river. I love the peaceful meandering of the Murray River and this day was no different. Birds were singing and the water was silent, except for the occasional splash when fish would flip out and then back into the river. At one point I looked at my watch. It was noon. If I wasn't at the river, I would almost certainly be with Day.

I got hungry and remembered that my bag was still at school. That was okay. A bit of hunger was nothing compared to what I could be dealing with.

I made a plan to pack a bag with some fishing gear and spare clothes, so I could do this regularly. Changing into spare clothes would mean my school clothes didn't get dirty, and also stop anyone being able to identify which school I was from and then report me.

I looked for a place to hide the bag, so I could leave it near the river. Eventually, I found a withered, large, hollow log. Perfect. It was then 2.30 and time to get the bus home.

Mum saw me arrive home without my bag and asked where it was. Quick as a flash, I told her I'd forgotten to bring it home, which she seemed to accept. I went to our shed and found an old bag and some fishing gear, which I stuffed into the bag. I then went to my room, grabbed some old clothes and went back to the shed, where I stuffed the bag fuller and left it there, ready for me in the morning.

CHAPTER SIX

A NEW FRIEND

I started skipping school and going to the river once or twice a week. It became my haven. I found a spot with low bushes and tall trees, where I was pretty much hidden from general view. The log was a great hiding place for my bag; for extra security, I fixed some bark over the exposed end.

The one thing I didn't have was bait to go fishing, but I used my initiative, which partly came from being part of the Boy Scouts. Dad had made me join a couple of years earlier to help make me more sociable. On the riverbank, I found an old dip tin, used for dipping grapes before they were dried. It was perfect for catching shrimp. I just needed to pack it with gum leaves to lure shrimp into the tin. My dad had hundreds of these tins at home, but I was glad I'd found one at the river because they weren't something that could be easily concealed on the school bus, and the last thing I wanted to do was draw attention to myself. Hooks and sinkers were no problem. Along the riverbank were plenty of cut lines with hooks and sinkers still attached. I was in business.

I loved being by the river so much, it was hard to drag myself away to catch the school bus home. I wanted to stay the night there. I would have had no more fear in the bush at night than in my bedroom. And at least when I stared up, I would see stars instead of a ceiling with people dressed in black floating around and gesturing at me to join them. Being by the river gave me the escape I needed. So long as I didn't get caught wagging school, I was alright.

Of course, my regular absences were going to attract the attention of Father Day. One morning he approached me in the school yard and asked where I'd been.

A NEW FRIEND

I had to think quickly. 'I've been sick, Father,' I said.

'What's been wrong with you?'

'The doctor didn't know.'

He told me he didn't believe me, grabbed the back of my jumper and dragged me to the presbytery. I knew what I was in for, but I had learnt that the quicker I let Day have his way, the quicker it was over.

'I've missed my special boy,' he said once we were inside, and proceeded to abuse me. When he'd finished, he told me to come over every Tuesday lunchtime, and if I didn't, it'd be a boys' home for sure.

For the next few days, the same feelings swirled around my head. I was at fault for the abuse. I must be. I was paying for my sins. One time, I overheard a visitor to our house telling Mum about a local man who had taken his own life because he had an incurable sickness. It put ideas into my head. I had heard drowning was a peaceful way to die and I imagined myself drowning in the river. I knew the Murray River often took good swimmers who found themselves out of their depth, so it would be easy for me.

Obviously, my schoolwork started suffering again. I kept getting told off for daydreaming. Even Sister Angela, the best teacher you could wish for, lost patience with me and sent me to a desk at the back of the classroom so she didn't have to deal with me. With some ninety kids in the class, I was soon forgotten back there. I didn't even care that I couldn't see the blackboard from there. It also helped me when I wagged, because it wasn't noticed; there were no roll calls. So long as the school got its fees, they were happy.

The first Tuesday after Father Day ordered me to always come and see him on Tuesdays, I decided I would spend the day at the river. On the way to school, instead of getting off at the school bus stop, I stayed on the bus with a few other passengers until the last stop before the depot, which was the stop closest to the river.

'Wait a minute young fella,' the bus driver said as I started down the steps. 'Why are you getting off here?'

I was getting used to thinking on my feet. 'I'm meeting my mum here. She's taking me to see the doctor.'

'Why didn't she bring you with her?'

I hadn't expected this. I was momentarily stunned. My mind was racing. I knew I had to get this right or he'd report me to the school. I kept slowly walking down the stairs, stepped onto the kerb, turned and said, 'It was too early for me when she left. She had other things to do in town first. She told me to wait here for her. If you wait, she'll be here soon. You'll see.'

It seemed to do the trick. 'Okay,' he said. 'I can't wait,' and he pulled out onto the road.

Father Day chased me up whenever I missed one of his sessions, but I became adept at lying, not just to him but also to my parents. I knew it was a sin but I couldn't care less. I didn't care about my soul and how many marks it had on it. I wrote in my journal, *I don't want to go to heaven, because the priest will be there.*

At the end of the year, I flunked my exams again. How could it be otherwise? I tried but my time and mind were taken up with what Father Day was doing to me. One afternoon, Sister Angela kept me back after the rest of the class had left, and gave me a letter to take home. She told me I was going to have to repeat grade four.

I waited until it was bedtime and then quietly slipped the letter to Dad, as I knew he wouldn't be as mad as Mum. I didn't have to wait long, though, before Mum stormed into my room and snatched the blankets that I had pulled up over my head. She went on and on about how I would never amount to anything in life unless I changed my ways.

However, unbeknownst to me, Mum went to the school and begged the Reverend Mother to allow me to go up a grade, just to see how I went. If I didn't measure up, I would go back down. The Reverend Mother agreed.

*

The following year, 1959, went by like the second half of the previous year. I had a different teacher, though: Sister Bridget, who was elderly and often didn't seem to be with it.

A NEW FRIEND

Father Day didn't summon me so often and I concluded that he was bluffing about sending me to a boys' home; he had plenty of opportunities to have done it by then.

I had become a natural at wagging school. I would get off the bus with the rest of the kids and then just keep walking to the river. No-one ever questioned me about it. By then, I'd created a great camp site, and even built myself a lean-to to protect me from rain or the sun. It was just up from the hollow log where I stored my gear.

One day, as I was walking along the riverbank looking for discarded scraps that might come in handy, I heard a voice. It startled me, as I rarely saw anyone near my area. I looked around and saw a lady sitting on a log. She was wearing a long dress with white socks and black shoes, and her long hair was pulled back with a rubber band.

'Hi. Sorry to frighten you. Are you looking for something?' she said.

'No. Err, yes.'

'Make up your mind. Are you or aren't you? It's okay. My name is Judy and yours is …?'

'John.'

She asked if I was fishing and a few other questions and then gestured for me to sit with her.

'Come on, I won't bite,' she said.

She told me she didn't live far away and that she came here often. I was surprised. I hadn't seen her before and told her so. Then I worried I'd said too much. I'd given away the fact that I was a regular here, and she would know that I should have been at school. Lucky I wasn't in my uniform; she wouldn't know which school I went to.

We talked some more, and as we did, I tried to work out how old she was. I reckoned she was about twenty, just a little older than Marlene. She never asked me about school, which I was relieved about. It may have been a sign that she understood me. Eventually, she told me she had to return a book at the library but that she'd be back next Wednesday if I was around. I didn't know what to say. I wanted to see her again, but I didn't want her to think I was here so often, so I just nodded. Then she took off.

I had a good feeling about Judy and started to think about next week. If I went to the river on Wednesday instead of Tuesday, Day might summon me on Tuesday. If I went both days, I could get caught for wagging, because two days in a row would be noticed, and I hadn't done two days in a row yet. If only there was a way.

That night, as Mum and Dad were in the lounge, I went to Dad's writing desk and found a document with Dad's signature. Then I got a writing pad and copied it over and over again (it was easy to copy; far easier than Mum's would have been), and when I was confident enough with it, wrote a letter:

> Dear Sister Bridget,
>
> As John has a doctor's appointment for tests, he won't be at school on Tuesday and Wednesday next week.

The first version wasn't good enough, so I did another and then another, and a few more until I figured the handwriting looked enough like that of an adult. Then I signed the final one with Dad's name, looked at it with pride, and sealed it in an envelope. Then I went outside and threw all my practice pages down our long drop toilet.

At school on Monday the following week, I gave the note to Sister Bridget. She put it on her desk and left it there until we were doing our religious instructions. I watched with trepidation as she picked it up, read it and placed it inside a book. I had no idea if it had worked or not. But at the end of the day, as I was leaving the classroom, she stopped me and said, 'All the best at the doctor, John.'

I woke the following morning to the sound of rain on the roof. It was going to be wet at the river, so I packed my raincoat and a spare pair of boots, and threw my journal into my bag, knowing there wouldn't be much fishing that day. Later, sheltering on the banks of the river, I wrote in my journal:

A NEW FRIEND

Dear journal

I feel so lonely. I have to keep these secrets to myself. If it wasn't for you journal I don't know where I would be. Father Day has murdered my innocence. He said, 'I love you.' What does he mean? If you love someone do you hurt them? I am starting to understand I've been sexually abused. Was Anna sexually abused? But Day wasn't there then, he wasn't in Mildura. Could there been another priest doing the same thing as what Day has done to me? Surely not. There's some altar boys who are not at school any more since Day's been here. Have they left because they have told their parents and I haven't? Is there more to this then I know journal? Was Sister Barnard involved somehow with Day? I am starting to think she was, why did she take me to Day? Why did she make me wait for Day at the confession box? It's all starting to make sense to me now journal.

As I was writing, the rain stopped but tears were running down my cheeks. I had never felt as bad as I felt on this day, and just wanted to walk into the river and not come back.
Later that day, I wrote:

Dear journal

I feel like shit what can I do please help me. My nightmares are bad I can't take them no more. I try to think of other things as I am going to sleep, but the nightmares keep coming back, they are horrible. I wake up horrified and I can't go back to sleep. I am so tired at school and I am getting into trouble for not doing my school work, and I know now I am not going to pass my exams this year. I'll be staying down for sure, then mum will be yelling at me again.

When I finished writing this, I broke down uncontrollably. I just wanted to die. I didn't want to be on this planet anymore. Even hell couldn't be this bad. For some reason, my feelings that day were even worse than when Father Day was abusing me.

I got up and started walking along the river when I heard someone singing out my name. I froze, thinking it might be a nun – or even worse, Day. I hid in the bushes and peered through the branches. I could see it was Judy, but I still had my school clothes on, so I clambered to my log, got my spare clothes, got changed, and dried my eyes.

'John. John. Is that you?'

Yes, it was definitely Judy but it was Tuesday, not Wednesday. Why was she looking for me? She had run past me and was now heading away.

'I'm over here, Judy,' I yelled, coming out of hiding.

She came over and asked if I was alright. I told her I was but she didn't believe me. 'I could hear you from the road,' she told me.

I didn't say anything. I didn't think anyone would have heard me. I was embarrassed that she had done so. Dad would have told me that 'men don't cry'.

Judy made me sit down and plonked herself close beside me.

'We were going to meet tomorrow,' I told her.

'I know. But I was walking to town and heard you. Are you okay?'

'Sure, go to town,' I said, still embarrassed that she had heard me crying.

But she didn't go anywhere. At that moment, nothing mattered to her except my welfare. She asked me to tell her what was going on.

As a child, how can you tell an adult, let alone a lady you don't know, that you've been sexually abused by a priest, or by any grown-up for that matter? They'd ask what he had done to me. How could

I say I hold his penis, I rub it for him, I have his semen all over me as he lies on me and plays with my private parts? Surely no-one would believe me. They would call me a liar. And if Father Day found out, he would get Jim Barritt or other detectives onto me and I would end up in a boys' home. So, I stayed silent.

Judy read the situation well. 'I was off to the library to change my books,' she said. They're in the basket of my pushbike up there.' She gestured toward the road. 'I'll ride there, get some more books, then come back and read to you. How about that?'

'Yep, I would like that,' I said.

Judy left. I walked to the river's edge and stared into the still, clear water. I could see my face, and my eyes were red raw. I washed my face in the cold water, so glad that Judy hadn't pressed me on what was wrong.

When she returned, Judy showed me a book she had borrowed. It was *Mildura Calling* by Alice Lapthorne. I found out later that Alice had been the librarian at Mildura Library and her father had been involved with the establishment of one of the early local newspapers, the *Mildura Cultivator*.

The book was fairly dry and a ten-year-old would not normally be interested in such a book, but the way Judy read it, adding her experiences and information about Mildura, brought the book alive.

From then on, we met regularly and Judy would always read to me. I think I learnt more from Judy, and from the scouts, than I did from school. From Judy I got knowledge about the way the world was; from the scouts, survival skills on living in the world.

The year sped by and exams were soon upon me again. Father Day was still abusing me but not as often, and only for about ten minutes each time. Besides, he was starting to get sick of me not being around or forgetting to meet him. 'I was there but you didn't see me,' was my regular response to him.

I still wrote in my journal every day, as if I was talking to someone. I wrote about Judy helping me on that hideous day when I was at my lowest and reading to me while I fished. I wrote that I wanted to be with Judy every day but knew that it was impossible. I didn't even understand how I was getting away with the couple of days a week I was wagging school.

I failed the year again, which was no great surprise, and again I asked if I could go to a state school, which Mum dismissed out of hand. When the exams were finished, I could have stayed home but I told Mum I wanted to keep going to school until classes formally finished for the year. Mum was surprised, but of course, I just wanted to see Judy before the holidays.

The part of the Murray where I sought solace and hung out with Judy.

CHAPTER SEVEN

STANDING UP FOR MYSELF

In 1960, I turned twelve and repeated grade six. I still had Sister Bridget as a teacher, and was getting attacked from all sides. At home, my parents were constantly hassling me; at school, I was being teased for being kept back; of course, there was also Father Day. I became angrier and angrier at other kids; being a farm boy, I was stronger than most and sometimes took advantage of this physically.

I had also started to realise that Father Day was a child abuser and that what he was doing was a crime. But what could I do? I knew he had the police on his side, and that some of the nuns knew what was happening but were protecting not just him, but their own positions, by keeping their mouths shut. In the meantime, children like me were being sexually abused.

What made things seem even worse was that at this time, Father Day was appointed Monsignor Day, just one rung below a bishop. As a result, Mildura became an important parish in Victoria. This just made him more and more untouchable in my mind.

Getting older made me more and more aware of what was happening, increasing my hopelessness. I had regular suicidal thoughts, horrific nightmares and intense anger. I had no thoughts for anyone else – with one exception. The only person I respected and loved at that time was Judy.

One day, in June 1960, I was sitting in my lean-to by the river in drizzling rain. I heard Judy shouting, 'John, are you here?'

'Yes Judy.'

She made her way over and told me that it was going to rain heavily, and to go over to her place. I was quite comfortable in my lean-to on days of extreme weather, hot or cold, sitting and writing in my journal, but Judy's offer was irresistible, and I accepted. I felt very comfortable with Judy, not threatened in any way.

Judy's place wasn't far away, just through the bush and across the road, probably only about fifty yards from the river. Her place was very small, and we settled in the kitchen at a table only two people could sit around. On the mantelpiece were packets of tea, coffee, Milo and sugar, not in marked tins like Mum had. Other groceries were in an old box in the corner of the kitchen. When she put the kettle on, I went for a wander. Off the kitchen was her bedroom, with an old wire bed like the ones Dad had in the pickers' hut. There was a large suitcase on the floor with clothes hanging over the open lid.

I wandered back to the kitchen and Judy handed me a cup of steaming tea. 'There, that will warm you up. Now, I'm going to have some toast. Would you like some?'

'Yes please.'

She picked up the toasting fork, and at the same time grabbed a book. 'Have you heard of Jules Verne?' she asked.

I shook my head.

She handed me the book. *Twenty Thousand Leagues Under the Sea*. 'We'll have our toast and then I'll read it to you. Listen to that rain. We're in a good spot today.'

It was pouring but inside was cosy. I felt safe. We pulled the kitchen chairs closer to the stove and ate our toast. Judy opened the oven doors to let the heat into the room, then began to read to me. Judy had read many books to me, on all sorts of subjects, but this was the first science fiction book and my imagination soared.

She read for a couple of hours and then stopped, telling me it was lunchtime. I grabbed my bag and started getting my sandwiches out, but she told me to put them away. 'We're having fish and chips today,' she said. I couldn't believe my luck.

The rest of the day flew. I wished I could have bottled it because it was the best day I had ever had.

I boarded the bus home at Eighth Street, and at Thirteenth Street the schoolkids got on. One of the boys from my class sat beside me and asked why I hadn't been at school. When I told him I'd been at the doctor, he said, 'Jeez, you go to the doctor a lot. How come?'

I told him it was none of his business, but he wasn't in the mood to stop.

'I'll make it my business,' he told me. 'My mum saw you going the wrong way to school the other day. Where were you going?'

'I told you, it's none of your business.'

'Well, I'm telling Sister on you tomorrow.'

That's all I needed, someone dobbing me into the nuns and then Father Day having something to hold against me. This boy had me worried.

'You're in the shit, Fitzy.' He laughed.

I lost it. I swung my elbow and hit him in the mouth, then pulled him down to the floor of the bus. 'Now listen, you fucking shithead,' I told him. 'You dob on me and you'll get a lot more of this. You hear me?' By this time, I had hold of his collar and tie and was twisting them, causing him to choke. I kept twisting. 'You dobbing on me?'

'No Fitzy,' he gulped.

I reluctantly let go. I wasn't certain he'd heed the warning.

The next morning, I didn't go to the back of the bus as I normally did; I stayed at the front so I could be first off. When the bus pulled up at the school stop, I raced ahead and hid in someone's garden. As the boy passed, I pulled him into the bushes, punched him in the stomach and pushed him onto the ground. I ground my knee into his chest.

'You remember what I told you last night, you shit?' I hissed, my face almost against his face.

He was scared. So scared. 'Yes Fitzy. I won't tell.'

At last, I believed him. I stood and left him lying in that garden.

I decided not to go to school that day. The rain had passed and the sun was out; it was a perfect day for fishing. Now that I knew where Judy lived, I decided to call on her and see if she wanted to come.

She was out the back hanging up her washing. She was pleased to see me but didn't want to go fishing, suggesting we take a walk along the river instead. Why not? I wasn't going anywhere else. She packed some food and we headed off.

We walked in silence for some time before Judy asked if I was alright. 'You seem to be in another world,' she said.

I told her I was fine and happy to be on the river with such a good friend, which delighted her.

We went into the bushland, towards the caravan park, and kept walking. When we got hungry, we stopped and unpacked lunch. As we ate, we chatted. She asked how our grapes were growing and how they were dried. I explained the process then told her my dream was to have my own fruit block when I was older. She told me about living in Melbourne and how she much preferred the country, but that one day she would have to go back to the city. I didn't want to hear that.

We got so caught up talking that I didn't realise how long we'd been there. By the time we got back to Judy's place, there was no way I was going to catch the normal bus home. The next one was an hour later, meaning I'd be very late. I sat on that bus coming up with excuses, as I knew Mum and Dad would be mad. But when I got home, they were still up on the block, pruning the vines. I went straight to my room and wrote in my journal.

Dear journal

It was a great day to go for a walk. The sky was as blue as blue and everything was so still. Even the kookaburras were having a laugh and the swallows were darting in and out of the trees and swooping the river. For some reason I feel real good, the best I have felt since Monsignor Day started assaulted me. Walking with Judy made all the difference. I feel I am getting more control of my life. My anger seems to help, and I should stand up to Day and call his bluff, I've got nothing to lose, I am nearly thirteen and it's time to stand up to him and the nuns and not take any shit from them.

*

The next day at school was my first in three days and I'd forgotten that we had confession first thing in the morning, and mass in the afternoon. Sister Bridget told the class she needed some children to help clean outside between confession and mass because someone had emptied the rubbish bins on the ground near the church.

She walked up and down the classroom aisle, tapping children on the shoulder with her strap. When she got to me, instead of tapping me lightly, she poked me with the stick that held the strap. Any hopes I'd had about missing confession and mass were gone. I was trapped.

As we walked over to the church, I thought about making a run for it but if I was caught things would be made worse for me. Entering the church, the familiar pain in my stomach and lump in my neck took hold.

When it was my turn for confession, I reluctantly walked into the box. To my relief, the silhouette was not that of Monsignor Day. As I knelt down, I started thinking about what I was going to say. 'Bless me Father, for I have sinned it's been a week since my last confession.'

'What sins do you have, my child?'

'I have no sins, Father.'

'You have no sins, my child?'

'That's right.'

There was silence. I wanted to tell him that it was Monsignor Day who had the sins but I held back.

'Say three hail Marys, my son,' he eventually said. Then he blessed me.

I felt so good about what I had done and, instead of kneeling when I left the box, I went straight to a seat and sat down. No-one said a word.

For the churchyard chores, I made sure I stayed on the side of the church furthest from the presbytery so Day wouldn't see me, but to no avail. I was bent over, picking up rubbish when I noticed him striding towards me.

'Where have you been, young man?' he said. 'I've been looking for you.'

I stood up and was almost looking him straight in the eyes. I hadn't realised it until that moment that I was almost as tall as Day. That gave me strength and courage. 'Why?' I asked.

'Have you forgotten our deal, Johnny?'

'It's not Johnny no more. It's John, I don't like Johnny.'

'Okay, John it is. Now come over to my rooms and we'll talk about it.'

'NO! I am not going anywhere with the likes of you.'

He was stunned. 'Don't talk to me like that.'

'I'll talk to you how I like.'

Then I walked away, while behind me, Day said, 'You'll be in a boy's home within a week, young man.'

I immediately regretted my response. I had called his bluff, but what if he went to his police mates and they looked into why I had missed so much school? It felt as if everything was about to close in on me. I started to experience paranoia. The other kids seemed to be looking at me, the nuns in black appeared to me as devils, and Monsignor Day stood there, hands on hips, glaring at me.

My anger rose higher than ever before. I hated everyone, even Judy. Why couldn't she see what was happening to me? I didn't have the guts to tell her, or anyone else for that matter. We were led back to school but I slunk away. I was going to go to the river but instead walked all the way home. It took me the rest of the day.

I sat up until late that night, writing in my journal. It helped to release my anger and fears, and I hoped it would mean I didn't have nightmares. Unfortunately, that wasn't the case. I had a nightmare in which Monsignor Day, the nuns and a pack of schoolkids were chasing me along the river. I was naked, except for heavy boots, and they were catching me fast. Judy was yelling at me to run faster. Then I was in the confession box with Day. There was no partition between us and he was standing with his pants down, his penis erect, telling me I have many sins. When I woke, my heart was racing, and my skin sweating. It was 5 am. As I moved, I realised

I had wet the bed. I got up and grabbed my journal, only to find it was full. I hid it in the wall and started a new one.

The weeks passed and I had no contact from Monsignor Day. I was relieved that the police hadn't been in touch either. I decided to study hard for the end of year exams. I really didn't want to repeat again. I cut my visits to Judy back to once a week. But it made no difference; I failed again.

With the exams over, the sixth-grade students went to school one day to prepare for first form. I hadn't been told that I would be repeating, I just assumed – so, I went to see Judy instead. I had told her I'd be along that day.

Judy was waiting by the road and looking out for me. She waved. 'Well, look at you,' she said. 'Don't you look smart with your uniform on.'

I looked down. 'I haven't changed my clothes yet.'

'That's okay, we're not fishing today.'

'Why not?'

'Because it's our Christmas today. Come into the house.'

Standing in a pot in the living room was a Christmas tree, a real one. She had probably cut the branch off a pine tree herself. It was decorated and at the bottom was a present for me.

I felt bad. 'I've got nothing for you, Judy.'

'I don't need anything, John. I've got all I want.'

The day turned out to be one I have never forgotten. She had made a Christmas lunch, and afterwards, she read to me. I felt wanted, loved and as happy as I had felt since the first time Day abused me.

CHAPTER EIGHT

GOODBYE FRIEND, GOODBYE SCHOOL

I started 1961 believing I would be repeating grade six, seeing as I had failed my exams again. But Mum had again talked to the Reverend Mother, and I was put into form one at St Joseph's College. No doubt Mum thought that it was because of her efforts, but I later found out it had been done to keep up the pass rate of the school, to make the school look good.

My teacher in form one was Sister Leo, whom I hadn't heard about. I was very distrustful of nuns by this stage and walked into class with the attitude that I wasn't going to take any shit from her. In hindsight, that was unfair because she was compassionate, quiet and, most unusually for the teacher nuns back then, didn't carry a strap.

I tried hard in form one but my frequent absences and lack of concentration in the past meant I found the work very hard. It didn't help that I still saw Judy whenever I could, often sneaking out of school when we got out for lunch, running to the river to see Judy and do some fishing.

I wrote about seeing Judy for the first time that year:

> Dear journal
>
> It was a Tuesday morning I left home early to catch the bus on the Calder highway an hour earlier than normal, this bus was normally for the workers in town as I was anxious to see her.

As I got to our spot Judy wasn't there. Seeing it was early Judy would be still at home so I went thought the bush across the road and knocked on her door I could hear footsteps and Judy opened the door.

'John it's great to see you. Wow you have growing since I last seen you. I can't believe you growing so much just in a few weeks.'

Then she gave me the biggest hug I ever had, it felt good, because I can't remember ever getting hugs from mum or dad as far as that goes.

I can hear dad saying, 'Don't make the boy a sook.'

There's no doubt that Judy was a lifesaver to me; she gave me a reason to live. I was becoming more and more of a loner, with depression and anger increasing, but my troubles seemed to go away when I was with Judy.

By then, Monsignor Day was leaving me alone physically but every now and again he would stand in the school yard and stare at me. I did all I could to avoid him. One Sunday morning, I told Mum I wasn't going to church anymore. She flipped.

'You're coming to mass and that's that, young man. Your schooling is disgraceful, you answer back … you must be mixing with the wrong children at school.'

She went on and on, so I gave in and went to mass.

Monsignor Day was giving the early mass as usual. Mum and I were sitting down the back so he couldn't see me, and an added bonus was the large person sitting right in front of me. His sermon that morning was about respect for others and respect for priests.

He described priests as being inferior to God, but superior to man, and that anyone who insults a priest, insults Christ.

When I heard that, I nearly fell off my seat, and must have made a noise because Mum gave me a glare that would have killed lesser beings. I made a note that this was definitely my last time at Sunday mass. When Mum got up to go for communion, she nudged me to go with her, but I said, 'No,' and walked outside. I remember thinking how easy it had been.

On the way home, Mum didn't say a word, though her face betrayed her thoughts. When we got home, I went to Dad's tobacco drawer and took out a packet of his Havelock fine cut tobacco, some cigarette papers and a box of matches. Then I walked up the block, sat on the channel bank and rolled a smoke. Thirteen, and I had started smoking.

One Monday morning in September that year, I walked into the school grounds and saw Judy by the gates, talking to Sister Pancratius. My heart stopped. I hid behind a fence and watched Judy poking her finger towards Sister Pan, as we called her. I didn't know what they were talking about, but it looked serious, and I assumed I was in trouble. I didn't know whether to run or stay put. Just as I was considering my options, Judy started to walk away, turned back, said something else to Sister Pan while pointing at her accusingly, then mounted her pushbike and rode off, leaving Pan standing there. I decided to go into school, but I was not happy with Judy. She must have been talking to the nun about me.

That morning, I was sitting, staring out the window when I heard Sister Leo calling. 'John. John. John Fitzgibbon.'

'Yes,' I finally responded.

'Come up here now and tell me what you're doing.'

I stood up, picked up my bag and started to walk out of the room.

'What are you doing?' she asked.

'I'm going for a piss then going home, what's it to you?'

And that's exactly what I did.

The following morning, I got up early to catch the workers' bus into town. I wanted to see Judy and ask what it had all been about the day before. I got to the spot where we regularly fished and Judy was already there with her line. She was surprised to see me so early.

I sat on the log beside her and she immediately put an arm around me, placed her head against mine, and squeezed me tight. Her eyes were glassy and there were tears in her bottom eyelids.

'Are you still leaving school when you're fourteen, like you told me?' she asked.

I nodded.

'What are you going to do?'

'Work on the block with my dad.'

'Well, you seem to know a lot about fruit blocks so that's great.'

We sat in silence for a while, then I asked, 'What were you doing at the school on Monday?'

Back to silence.

Finally, she responded. 'John, there's some things that should be let go and left for others to take care of. You are in my heart at all times and always will be.' Then, she jumped up. 'I'll be back in a moment. I just have to get something from the house.'

It was some time before she came back, and if there really was something she had gone to fetch, she came back empty-handed. She had clearly been crying though. I didn't ask her any questions and she said little for the rest of the day. Of course, I was puzzled, but happy to leave it. We caught about six fish and cooked a cod for lunch. After lunch, we walked along the river to the caravan park, then cut though the bush back to Judy's house. By then, it was time for me to make tracks to the bus. I left none the wiser as to what Judy had been doing at school.

The next day in class, Sister Leo told me that Sister Pancratius wanted to see me. I could be in trouble for wagging school, or walking out on Sister Leo or whatever Judy was doing there. I guessed I was about to find out. When I arrived at Sister Pan's room she sat me down, closed the door behind me, and then took a seat behind her desk, looking straight at me. 'Now young man, what's going on with you?' she said.

'Why?'

'Don't use that tone of voice with me. Just answer me. What's going on?'

'Nothing.'

She sighed in frustration and raised her voice. 'There's something wrong and if you don't tell me I'll take you …'

I didn't let her finish what she was going to say. I knew she was going to say – she'd send me to Monsignor Day.

'Like fuck you will, YOU BITCH,' I yelled, staring straight back at her and holding up a fist. I then stood, grabbed my chair and hurled it against the wall. I looked at her one last time and walked out of the school, past the presbytery – willing to hit Day if he was outside, which he wasn't – and towards the river. In hindsight, I don't think she was going to tell Monsignor Day; I don't know what she was going to say. But I didn't give her a chance to explain. I just lost it, that's how my mind was at the time.

As I walked along Eleventh Street, a car pulled alongside me and slowed down. I saw Detective Jim Barritt driving. He looked worried, panicked even. He drove past, then turned around and came back towards me. I just kept walking, making out I hadn't seen him, and he too kept going. At the time, I wondered whether he had been sent by Day, who had heard what had happened in the classroom, or if he just happened to be driving past. Later, I considered another option, given what I found a half hour or so later, and the look on his face.

I had decided I was going to tell Judy my story. I needed to tell someone. But she wasn't home. I went to our fishing spot but she wasn't there either. I walked up and down the river looking for her but finally gave up and went to my log. There, stuck to the log, was a note, scrawled on a piece of paper and placed on top of a *Women's Weekly* magazine:

> Hello John, I am sorry but I must go home. You can have my fishing gear; you will be leaving school soon. All the best.
>
> I'll look you up one day. All my love, Judy x.

I was shattered. More than shattered. My best friend had gone and didn't wait around for me, to say goodbye. I walked back to her house, just in case I had missed her the first time around. I yelled out, knocked on the back door, peered through the window, but there was no sign of her. I went back to the river and cried for Judy for the rest of the day. Later, I wrote a poem in my journal:

> Always back in time to catch the bus.
>
> Never found out this will do.
>
> Met a lady on the river we fished together it's great.
>
> She read to me while we fished.
>
> She never asked, why aren't you at school?
>
> Over a full term I had knowing the lady.
>
> She left a note. Keep my rod.

I never saw Judy again, though I thought of her often. I still have her rod, her fishing bag and the magazine. I believe she met with foul play, and that Monsignor John Day and Detective Senior Sergeant Jim Barritt had something to do with it. There is no evidence for my theory, but Barritt's demeanour when he drove past me could have been a result of disposing of Judy. Hers wouldn't be the only body dumped into the Murray. And given I had never seen her handwriting before, who's to say she even wrote that note? I believe she knew what was going on; that's what her conversation with Sister Pancratius was all about. Perhaps Sister Pan even passed on details of her conversation, raising the alarm in church and police circles?

Many years later, when the Church was finally held to account in the district, Sister Pancratius made her one and only statement about the situation, published in the *Mildura Sunday Independent* on 9 October 2005. She said, 'Things had been going on for a long time and something had to be done about it.'

*

School changed a lot for me after Judy had gone. Amazingly, I was never held to account for my outburst at Sister Pancratius. Maybe she knew what was going on, felt for me, and didn't tell anyone.

Almost everyone just stayed away from me, which suited me fine. That could have had something to do with another incident one morning at assembly. A boy kept poking me in the back, and persisted even after I told him to stop. Sister Leo turned to see what the commotion was and at that moment, I clenched my fist and punched him in the nose. He fell to the ground, blood spurting from his nose. Sister Leo just turned and went into the classroom. She never said a word. No-one did. In the past, Monsignor Day would have been told, but I never saw him. I didn't see him for months. Maybe things were starting to get a bit hot for him and the creep was staying indoors.

Obviously, my anger and depression were still with me. Some days were not so bad, but on others it was like being sucked into a black hole. If I wasn't happy on a particular day, I would still go to school and just do pretty much as I liked. As for the river, I only went there a few times. With Judy gone, it was no longer my happy place.

Towards the end of first form, it was decided that a swimming pool would be built for the nuns. They asked for volunteers to help with the digging and to push wheelbarrows full of dirt up a ramp. It was typical of the school and church; get what it could for free, even if was virtual slave labour. I didn't put my hand up for that.

On Wednesday 1 November 1961, two weeks before my fourteenth birthday, I walked out of school for the last time. I hadn't woken up that morning intending to leave school, but during the morning, Sister Leo said something to me that prompted my actions. Amazingly, I can't remember what she said but I opened my desk, got my bag out and emptied the contents of my desk into the bag. The kid next to me asked what I was doing and I replied, 'I am fucking off out of this shit hole.' It was loud enough for the whole class to hear. I walked up to Sister Leo and looked her in the eye. She had the saddest face, seemingly full of remorse, and as I walked past her, she gave me a nod. Surely another one who knew what was going on. I walked out of the classroom, past Sister Pancratius's class, past the presbytery and church, and never went back.

I went down to the river, sat on my log and stared across the river. I recalled the good times Judy and I had together. I had mixed emotions. I didn't regret what I had done. I was the happiest I had been since Judy left – but her absence still made me sad.

I stayed at the river until late in the afternoon. I had missed the school bus, so I was in no hurry. I took all the fishing gear out of the log, as well as Judy's note and bag, and tried to cram them all into my school bag. They wouldn't fit, so I took out some of my schoolbooks and put them in the log so the other stuff would fit. Then I went over to my lean-to and sat there for a while, processing everything. I started to feel numb, as if my life was over.

I finally got a late bus home, and I must have been a sight – a boy in school uniform with a fishing rod and a heavy bag overflowing. I got a few strange looks.

I got home just as Mum and Dad were walking back to the house from working in the vines, so I hid Judy's things in the shed and went to my room to write in my journal. I had four journals by this time and they were a mess. They were full of drawings: of a black box with a boy kneeling and a priest looking though a little window; shapes of my nightmares; swear words telling the priest and nuns where to go. And there were plenty of torn pages. They were the journals of a very angry boy.

That night, I wrote:

> Dear journal
>
> I have left that shit hole. No more priest for me, no more nuns, no more school, no more church. They can all get fucked. But did I miss my chance by not waiting for sister Pancratius too, to get her to explain what was on her mind? Should I have told her my story? Would she have believed me? Is that why she asked for me? Did Sister Leo know what

was happening as well? I think I missed my chance to tell, but then if no one believed me, I could have been in big trouble, so I'll leave it as it is. Now dear journal I haven't told mum and dad that I've left school. I'll do that tonight.

Journal ends of my school days.

At teatime that night, I told Mum and Dad that I had left school and that I'd work on the block. To my surprise, Dad just said, 'I want you to put the cultivator on the tractor in the morning and cultivate the middle patch for me, please.'

Nothing was said about school.

The items Judy left behind. Who leaves their handbag behind? Just one more puzzle I have never solved. I never saw her again.

CHAPTER NINE

BECOMING A MAN

School may have been behind me, but my nightmares and depression remained. I wasn't able to leave them behind me, so I learnt to put them alongside me. Keeping busy was a key to coping. I worked with Dad, went on walks organised by the Department of Agriculture, and also put a lot of effort into my scouting.

Over the years, the Boy Scouts had become a haven from the abuse and depression. I loved camping and fishing, and the scouts taught me great survival skills. In 1962, I became a scout leader and went on two jamborees, one in the Dandenong Ranges and the other in Perth. The jamborees gave me exposure to scouts from all around the world. I saw there was a great deal more to life than Mildura.

In 1963, I started night school to study engineering. It was something I had always wanted to learn but it wasn't taught at a Catholic school. One of my main motivations was to be able to repair Dad's equipment instead of Dad having to pay someone to fix it.

It was a one-year course and we had just two weeks to go when there was a change in teacher. The new teacher knew his stuff and was very jovial, but he was always touching people. He would walk past and run his hands over your back and things like that. He didn't mean anything by it, but it got too much for me and I left a week before our exams. Once you've been the victim of sexual abuse, it doesn't take much to tip you over the edge. Once again, Monsignor Day had gotten the better of me.

About this time, my nightmares got worse, I fell into a deep depression and was smoking a pack a day to cram my nerves. I felt that Mum had been right about me not amounting to anything. Not good, not fair, for someone in their mid-teens.

All this coincided with puberty and my hormones kicking in. I'd had no sex education at school or at home, so I had no idea what was happening to me. I thought my brain had gone haywire. I'd wake in the mornings with an erection, which did nothing but remind me of Father Day making me hold his penis and rub it until it was stiff, then wet and sticky. I started to think I was going to be as bad as him. Thoughts of suicide re-entered my mind.

There was no Judy to help me now, but what saved me was the scouts. Once a month, we would go camping and perform tasks towards our Queen Scout Badge. One night, around the campfire, our scout leader gave us a sex education talk. Later, in the tent, the boys continued the chat. We strayed well beyond what the scout master had said, and I'm sure lots of what we were talking about wasn't accurate, but the most important thing was that I found out I was normal as other boys.

When everyone fell asleep that night, I got up and went walking through the bush. There was just enough moonlight for me to see where I was treading. The knowledge that I was like all other boys filled me with so much joy and cemented in my mind that Father Day was the evil one – a child molester and monster.

There was a constant, nagging thought I had as I wandered through the bush; there must be others suffering what I suffered at his hands. If so, what should I do? If I did nothing, surely that would make me as bad as Day. One of the things holding me back was that I didn't know whom to talk to. From what I had seen, the police were on his side. I thought of Anna, always crying, and believed that she had also been abused. Old memories came flooding back and I felt the bile rising in my body until I doubled over and vomited.

*

In February 1964, when I was sixteen years old, it was fruit harvest time and Dad gave me more responsibility. Chief among those duties was supervising the pickers and the cartman. Back then, the grapes were picked by about ten pickers, and then two workers would spread them out on wire netting, known as drying racks. Later, they were transported by a cartman. We had all sorts of people work for us as pickers, from Queensland cane cutters to university students from all over Australia.

One picker stood out to me over all the others. Her name was Barbara, and she was eighteen years old, about five foot ten, with long hair and a divine figure. She wore a black ribbon to tie her hair back, so it wouldn't get caught up in the vines. What took most of my attention was that she always wore a tight white T-shirt and shorts, and never wore a bra.

Barbara was from Mildura but studying at university in Melbourne. She came home on her holidays to see family and earn money picking fruit. She drove a blue MG sports car that her brother lent her to drive between Mildura and Melbourne. Whenever she had trouble with her car, which was fairly often, I helped to fix it. Occasionally, she would let me drive it around the roads near home.

One day it was so hot, about 48°C, that we let the pickers knock off work. She told me she was going to the river for a swim and asked if I wanted to go with her. Now, that was an offer I couldn't refuse. We jumped into the MG and off she shot, the wheels spinning in the dust.

When we got to the river, she raced out of the car, straight to the river, and dived in. She stayed under far too long for my liking but just as I began to think something had happened to her, her head broke the surface. She swam to the riverbank, and I told her off for not checking how deep the water was, or whether there was a log or any other obstacles in the water. She was bemused by my concern but after I told her she could have ended up in a wheelchair, she agreed and thanked me for my concern. In fact, she said, 'You're lovely,' which sent a thrill through me.

I joined her in the water and swam along the river to find some shade. We sat on a submerged log and talked. She told me about living in a flat in Melbourne with other university students, which was almost as alien to me as living in another country. After all, I had only been to Melbourne once. But most memorable of all was the sight of her breasts through her soaking T-shirt. I'm sure she knew what I was looking at. After a couple of hours of talking and splashing each other to keep cool, she drove me home.

The following day was just as hot, only it brought with it a huge thunderstorm. As the dark clouds approached, it was all hands on deck covering the fruit so it wouldn't get ruined. As we were racing around, I looked for Barbara but couldn't see her. I realised she was still on the block and told Dad I'd pick her up on the tractor.

I hurried because a storm like that, after such heat, almost always meant hailstones the size of golf balls. Just as I pulled up in the row next to where Barb was, it began pouring.

'Quick, under the trailer,' I yelled at her.

I jumped off the tractor and scuttled under the trailer. In the few seconds it took, it not only started raining, but I got drenched.

I waited for Barb to scuttle under, but the seconds ticked, the rain poured, and there was no sign of her. In fact, there was no sign of almost anything. Visibility was down to a few metres and the noise on the trailer was deafening. Just as I was shuffling out to go and find her, Barb dived under the trailer.

'That's fucking heavy rain,' she said, 'and I got hit by hail.'

She was rubbing her forehead and I could see a lump already. Then I turned my gaze downward and again looked at her drenched T-shirt. This time Barb didn't ignore my stares.

'Do you like what you see John?' she asked.

I was so embarrassed. 'Sorry, sorry, I didn't mean to.'

'Don't be sorry. I don't mind. I'm taking it off anyway as it's sticking to me.'

And with that, she took her top off.

For the first time in my life, I was gazing at naked breasts. She then grabbed one of my hands, placed it on one of her breasts, and started kissing me. She was experienced, that's for sure. There was no shyness, no uncertainty from her. She started kissing me all over my body, put her hands inside my pants and pulled them off. Within seconds she was on top of me, bouncing up and down, occasionally hitting her head on the trailer, while I just lay there. By the time we'd finished, the hail had stopped, the rain was easing, and we were covered in mud. We slid out from under the trailer, and stood naked in the rain, helping each other get the mud off. When we got back to the drying racks, everyone had gone. Barb just dropped me off and told me she had to go to the shops for her mum – as nonchalantly as that.

As I got inside, Dad was doing some bookwork. He looked up and asked me, 'How did the fruit look on the vines as you were coming back?'

'It seems to be alright,' I told him, but to be honest, I hadn't looked. My mind had been somewhere else altogether.

Lying in my bed that night, I had mixed feelings. It had felt good with Barb, but I kept getting flashbacks of Monsignor Day. I finally fell asleep but had a nightmare in which I was doing to Day what I had done with Barb. Day had a sickly laugh and a revolting smile, and though I knew it was a dream, I couldn't wake out of it. I was yelling, 'Let me out, let me out,' loud enough for Mum and Dad to come in my room and wake me. I told them I'd had a nightmare but neither of them asked what it had been about. I wouldn't have told them if they had.

It was still night-time, not even the early hours of the morning, so I got up, crept outside, and went to the shed to get the tobacco I hid there, then wandered up to the block. I had to pass the house of the Italian neighbour who Dad drank with, as Mum wouldn't allow Dad to drink at home. The neighbour didn't speak much English, but we always managed to understand each other. He loved playing practical jokes on us, like hiding in the bushes and throwing dirt clods at us or pulling the pin out of the trailer so we would drive off without it. He was in his fifties but a kid at heart.

When I got to his house, I decided to see if he was up. I knocked on his door but there was no answer. I went around to his shed, where Dad and he drank. He wasn't there either, but his bar fridge was. I grabbed three bottles of Melbourne Bitter and took them to the channel, where I sat on the bank, knocked the top off one of the bottles with my pocketknife, and rolled a cigarette. I didn't consider I had stolen the beer because Dad put beer in Joe's fridge each week.

As I never got paid from Dad for working on the block, I figured it evened itself out.

So, there I was at sixteen, drinking, smoking and having had my first sexual encounter with a woman, all on the same day. After a couple of the bottles of beer, and a few smokes, I was feeling on top of the world. I decided not to wreck the feeling I had, so hid the third bottle in the channel, under a bridge, so it would stay cool.

The next morning, as the pickers arrived for the day's work, I was getting the tractor ready when Barb came up beside me. 'John, about yesterday,' she said. 'My boyfriend is coming up this arvo from Melbourne. Please be careful what you say.'

That was news to me. I didn't know she had a boyfriend. 'Why didn't you tell me?' I said.

'There was no point.'

She told me that what happened was between her and me, and to keep it that way. Then she drove off, leaving me bewildered. I lent on the tractor, thinking about the time Dad told me, 'You can't work woman out.' Now I understood what he meant.

Putting women out of mind, I concentrated on getting my Queen Scout Badge, which I did towards the end of the year. It gave me a great deal of satisfaction and confidence, and I went to Melbourne to receive the award from the Governor-General. Around the same time, I became a senior scout, and then an assistant scout master. What a way to end the year.

*

Unfortunately, the next year did not start so well. I began having panic attacks at night. They were so bad at times that I could feel my heart missing beats, and I broke out in cold sweats. For the first time, I went to see a doctor without my parents knowing, and it was a different doctor to the family doctor.

As soon as I walked into his room, he said, 'You're a smoker, aren't you?' I must have looked puzzled that he knew, so he explained, 'I am too, but I haven't had one for a while and can smell it on you.'

With that, he went to his desk, pulled out a packet of cigarettes, opened his window and lit up. He told me I could do the same, so

I got my packet of rollies out. When he saw what I was doing, he insisted I just take one of his. Finally, he told me to call him Bob and asked what I was there for.

I told him about my panic attacks. As he held a stethoscope to my chest and asked me to take deep breaths, he asked if I had any ideas about what was bringing the attacks on. I paused and then, for the first time, told someone about Father Day. He sat back in his chair and allowed me to talk. He listened intently to every word and when I was finished, he said, 'You're not the first to tell me this story. There are others in this town.'

I wasn't shocked; I knew there must have been. But what he said next did shock me.

'I'm afraid the Church is too strong,' he said. 'I can give you some tablets to help you sleep but there's not much more I can do. Your heart is okay, you're fit, just take the tablets.'

I didn't buy the tablets he prescribed. All I took from him was the knowledge that there was no help out there, no support, no-one I could talk to; I was going to have to deal with this by myself.

My drinking got heavier from then on. I regularly took cigarettes from Dad's tobacco drawer and beer from Joe's fridge, and sat on the bank of the channel, slowly getting wasted. I managed to hide it from everyone until a friend who lived close by found a few empty port bottles and figured they were mine, given where he found them. I guess I hadn't hidden them as well as I thought I had. He confronted me about them, but I got him onside by asking him to drink with me. We sat on the bank and drank a bottle of port each, then spent hours sobering up before heading home.

It soon got to the point that I was drinking about four bottles of port a week. For some reason, the pub sold port cheaper than normal on Saturday afternoons, so I would pop in after playing football or going to scouts, park my bike out of sight so the bar staff didn't see it, and buy four bottles. I was seventeen. I hid most of the bottles in the channel but always kept one in my bedroom. I found that if I drank a quarter of a bottle before going to bed, I wouldn't have nightmares.

One of my proudest moments was receiving the Queen's Scout Badge Award (me on left).

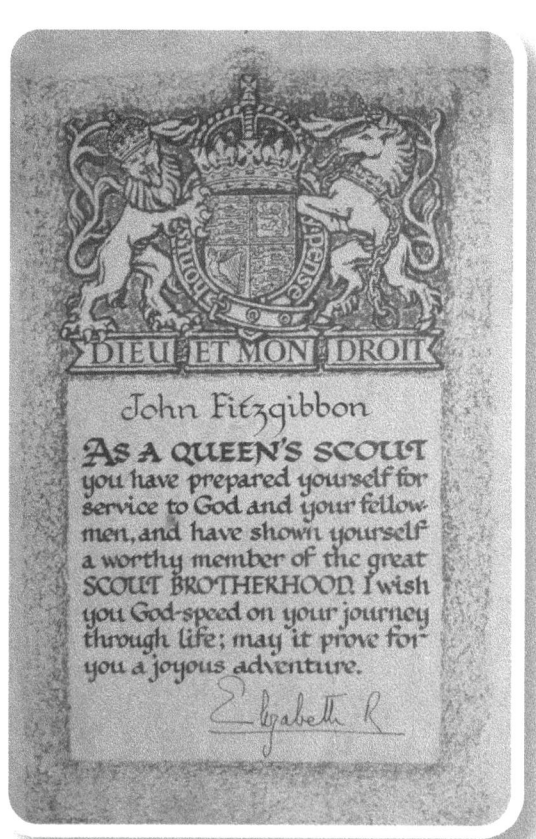

The award with Queen Elizabeth's signature.

CHAPTER TEN

PANDORA'S BOX

For some time, Dad had promised to buy me a car when I turned eighteen. In April 1966, eight months before my eighteenth birthday, I asked if I could have it early. To my astonishment, he agreed, even though I didn't have my driving licence yet.

Dad bought me a black FC Holden with a white top but told me that until I had my licence, I could only drive it on the block, not on the roads. I did as he said for a very short time, driving through the block to my mate's place. But soon, I was driving it on the road. Deceiving my parents felt good; it gave me a sense of power. I guess it was my way of getting back at the world for what happened to me.

It became a regular thing for me to drive through the block, pick up my mate from scouts, and then drive into town. Back then, it was 6 o'clock closing time in Victorian pubs, so we would cross the border into New South Wales, which had 10 o'clock closing. I never once got picked up for drink-driving. I don't think anyone did back then.

On Saturday nights, we would drink at the pub, get half-cut, and then go to the local dance. My friends would dance but I still had anger and frustration issues, so instead of enjoying myself like everyone else, I'd often get myself involved in a fight outside. The alcohol didn't help.

For eight months I drove without a licence, usually drunk. I partied, brawled, and sped along the roads at deadly speeds. I found this an exhilarating release. How I never killed anyone is beyond me. I stopped having nightmares, and, as a result, thought I was in control. In fact, I was out of control.

My eighteenth birthday fell on a Sunday, and the following morning Dad and I went to the police station to get my driving licence. I had gotten my tractor driving licence at fourteen, which was the practice back then, and the police officer who had tested me for that was the same one to test me for my driving licence. He got me to drive around the block once, asked me two questions, filled in a form and gave me my license.

I had my license, but my behaviour didn't change, at least not for a while. Then, one Saturday night, a friend of mine, Ken, pulled alongside a mate and me as we chatted by the roadside. Ken asked if we wanted to go with him down to the river. We told him we had other plans. At about 2 am, we got the news that Ken had driven his car into a tree, not far from where Judy and I used to hang out, and he was dead. Four others, who had been in the car, had been taken to hospital in a bad way. He was only eighteen, may he rest in peace. I knew that could have been me.

That incident helped sober me up, but what helped even more was falling in love. I had known Sheryl from scouting social events, and we started going out. Now, I was gaining happiness from something other than a bottle of booze, and I didn't want to blow it. I stopped going to wild parties, picking fights and drinking. I even gave up scouts, so I'd had more time for Sheryl. However, as close as we were, I held back from telling her what had happened to me at school.

One day, in October 1967, Sheryl rang me, upset. She told me to go around to her place, as she wanted to talk, now. I told her I'd be there in ten minutes but was there in five. I could see immediately that she'd been crying. I hugged her and asked what was wrong.

'I'm pregnant,' she said.

We talked it over and decided to tell our parents. I didn't want to tell Mum and Dad at the same time, so waited until they were in different rooms and told Dad first. He took it okay. Not so Mum.

'I knew you wouldn't amount to anything,' she said. 'Now you've got a girl pregnant, and this fruit block can't support two families. What are you going to do? What are people going to think?'

'I'll get a job and rent a house,' I told her, and then walked up to the block to get away from Mum and to consider the situation.

On my way up there, I started feeling like shit. Mum had put me down again, just like she had during my time at school. I could feel the depression starting to weigh on me. I looked around for something to do and noticed a strainer post at the end of a row needed replacing. So, I started digging a post hole and just kept digging, way too deep. By the time I finished, I couldn't put a post in there, but I sure felt better. I then went back to the house, got changed, and went for a drive to clear my mind.

Sheryl and I went out that night, but unbeknownst to us, our parents were meeting to discuss the situation. We found out they had a massive blue over religion, as Sheryl's family was Methodist. Apparently, despite his loathing for the Church, Dad told Sheryl's parents, 'If they don't get married in the Catholic Church, I won't help them in any way.'

As a result, we were told we were getting married in a Catholic Church, and for that to happen, Sheryl would have to convert. With Monsignor John Day still in Mildura, I pleaded not to have Day officiate at our wedding, but it fell on deaf ears. I suggested to Sheryl that we elope, but she took it as a joke. It was no joke.

For Sheryl to covert, she needed to be educated in the Catholic ways. An appointment was made for her first session. As we turned up at the presbytery that day, I started feeling as I had so many times before; my stomach churning and a lump developing in my dry throat. I didn't want to be there and felt as if my family had betrayed me by insisting that this was the way it had to be.

I rang the bell and after a few moments could hear footsteps. Standing there was a priest I didn't recognise. I was so relieved, but was still shaking and feeling anxious. We were shown into a room, and then Sheryl was escorted into another room, alone. Just a couple of minutes later she came scuttling out in tears.

I grabbed Sheryl's hand but she just brushed it away and stormed out. As I followed, I turned back to the priest and said, 'You fucking shithead. You can stick your fucking Church up your fucking arse.'

I had no idea what had happened to Sheryl, but I wasn't going to put up with my wife-to-be being put through whatever it was. I reckon I could have killed that priest that day.

Neither of us spoke on the car trip back to her parents' house. I dropped her off and drove home, hitting the steering wheel with my fist and yelled obscenities at the Church. Would I ever be rid of it? I drove so fast, and took corners so tightly, that I could smell the burning rubber from the tyres and the brake linings when I pulled up.

I went straight up to the block where Dad was working and told him that the priest had Sheryl in tears and that I didn't want anything to do with the Church. To my surprise Dad said, 'Okay, we don't need that bullshit. I don't care where you get married, but it won't be there.'

I needed that support from Dad right then.

Sheryl never told me exactly what the priest said, but I guessed it probably had to do with having a child out of wedlock, and sins.

The following week I found a job at the pub from which I had bought my port. A few days later, I found us a house on top of a hill by the main channel. It had an outside toilet, a can job some forty yards from the house, and no town water – just river water from the channel into tanks – but Sheryl liked it. I knew the owner and he wanted to help us out, so the rent was only three dollars a week.

On 29 November 1967, we got married in a Methodist Church in Mildura, followed by a budget honeymoon at Glenelg, South Australia, where we stayed in a rented caravan and never went anywhere as we were broke. Some months later, after pressure from my family (particularly Mum), we got married again, but in a Catholic Church. It was a quiet ceremony, with no sign of Monsignor Day, and no need for Sheryl to undergo any Catholic education. Sheryl's family was not told about this second wedding.

Our first child, Peter, was born in June 1968. Suddenly I was a family man with responsibilities. Around this time, my nightmares started again, and I tried to cope by working as hard as I could to keep my mind off my past. I put my hand up for as much overtime at the pub as I could get. Unfortunately, all the work did not shake off my depression. I kept it hidden from everyone, which in hindsight was not the best coping mechanism.

Sheryl was a great wife and mother, and we had our second child, Shane, in December 1969. By then I had two regular jobs, at the pub and as a local tanker driver, and also worked on fruit blocks around the area when I could. This kept my mind busy and my depression at bay; I tired myself out so I would sleep deeply, without nightmares. Sometimes it worked, sometimes it didn't; if there was a problem at home, I would spiral into depression. I tried to keep my depression to myself but, of course, Sheryl knew something was wrong. Because I wouldn't tell her what, she thought she was the problem. But she wasn't. She was my wife; I should have told her about Father Day and the abuse. But I didn't.

Things got so bad that I turned to the grog again, but this time I recognised the damage it could do. I made an appointment to see a doctor, a different one from before. I immediately felt comfortable with him; there was something about his manner. He appeared confident and clever, and I found myself telling him about my depression and Father Day and school and everything else I could think of. It was more like a counselling session, and I spilled my heart and soul to him.

When I'd finished, emotionally exhausted, he simply said, 'Get over it. It's been years, so why hang on to the past? There's nothing that can be done about it now. You should have spoken up then, and maybe there wouldn't have been other children abused.'

He wrote me a prescription, which I snatched from him, screwed up in front of his face, and threw in the bin.

I left in a rage, and only after I'd calmed down did I consider what he had said to me. How many children had been sexually abused after me? Was I as bad as Day for not speaking up? Were there now other adults suffering the same thoughts as me? And if so, was it my fault?

While working in the pub brought in money, access to easy alcohol was a problem. I worked the night shift, getting home around one or two in the morning, and then drank instead of going to bed. My other job started at 7.30 am, so it was hardly a healthy lifestyle. Sheryl put up with it all; she was quite the trooper. She tried to find out the cause of my problems, but I kept it all to myself.

I worked hard and was always scheming of ways to make money. Somehow, it seemed to pay off, at least financially. We built a home and took on the lease of a motel, while I maintained all my other work. I think I was trying to prove something to my parents – particularly Mum, who had constantly told me I'd amount to nothing. But at the same time, it was driving Sheryl mad, and I was pulled between impressing my parents and pacifying Sheryl.

In 1973, Dad sold the fruit block. He hadn't told me it was up for sale, and the papers were signed before I found out. I wasn't happy, as I was in a position to buy it and would have loved to have done so. However, over the months of settlement, the deal fell through, and I stepped in, buying the property from Dad. True to his word about not helping us out if we didn't marry in the Catholic Church, even though we had a second wedding there, he made me pay full market price. However, I put that aside. I saw no point holding a grudge. I was now a fruit grower. I had achieved one of my dreams.

One of the first things I did was plant a peppercorn tree. They grow quickly; within a few years it provided shade and solace for me. It was where I often went to deal with the demons in my mind, the haunting memories of Day and his abuse, the difficulties I had in forming in maintaining relationships. My visits to the tree were frequently accompanied with alcohol. I'm not sure whether I deliberately planted the peppercorn tree for this purpose, but it helped to replicate the sense of comfort I sought up in the peppercorn tree between the presbytery and the school, all those years before.

It was around this time that I found out that Monsignor Day had left Mildura the year before, and that he was alleged to have sexually assaulted several children in the area. When the news hit town about his abuse, there was uproar, with the town divided between those who believed the allegation and those who dismissed them. There was word that there may have been up to fifty victims. It turned out to be upwards of two hundred.

I was twenty-six years old when I heard the news, and I went straight up to the block and cried for those children. Yes, it was affirmation that he was evil, and that I was an innocent victim. However, I couldn't get the doctor's words out of my mind: 'You should have spoken up then.'

I felt guilty, then and still now, that I didn't speak up early enough to have stopped some of that abuse. It only takes one person to make a difference, but I wasn't that person. However, the more I think about it, Judy may have been that person. I believe she might have been trying to do something, enough to attract the attention of the Church – and Detective Jim Barritt or his cronies, who took matters into their own hands.

John Day's activities apparently came to light in 1971, when John Howden, deputy headmaster at St Joseph's College, Mildura, reported to Detective Denis Ryan that a 12-year-old girl alleged that she had been indecently assaulted by Monsignor Day. Detective Ryan started investigating and managed to collect sixteen damning written statements from students and former students, most of them male. In their statements, they testified that Day had driven them to Melbourne and molested them in his car, in his sister's house and in country motels along the trip.

Even as news spread around town, Mildura's *Sunraysia Daily* newspaper published nothing about it. Was George Tilley, the newspaper's editor from 1956 to 1988, warned not to publish anything, and even instructed his staff not to?

For his efforts in investigating Day and cover-ups in the Church, Detective Ryan was ordered to transfer to Melbourne, but he refused and instead resigned, forfeiting a large amount of his financial entitlements. Here was a man of principle punished for fighting corruption. The tentacles of the Church spread far and wide. So far, in fact, that an officer from Victoria Police Internal Affairs gave the Ballarat bishop, Ronald Mulkearns, a virtual heads-up: move Day or he would be charged. Using Church funds, Day was sent to Portugal, out of harm's way.

In State Parliament in March 1972, on two occasions, Les Shilton MLA (a former detective) told the Victorian Legislative

Assembly that pressure had been brought to bear by the Church on the police force and the Police Minister's department. He objected to Monsignor Day being allowed to leave Australia and urged the government to appoint a Supreme Court judge to conduct an inquiry into the matter. However, nothing came of it. In fact, when Monsignor Day eventually returned to Australia, despite the sixteen signed statements and the mentions in State Parliament, Day was rewarded with an appointment in the rural parish of Timboon, near Warrnambool, where he lived until he died in 1978. A eulogy of him was published in the Ballarat diocesan magazine, *The Light*.

With Pandora's Box well and truly open, throughout the town and in my mind, anger built up inside me, particularly when I overheard people having a beer and dismissing the rumours. The younger me would have turned my anger into something physical, but the more mature me left them at it and went home.

CHAPTER ELEVEN

THE HEALING PROCESS

By 1980, Sheryl and I were doing well financially. We had purchased a property next door and now had sixty acres of grapevines. It meant working long hours, seven days a week, but that's what I wanted: to keep occupied.

In early August that year, I was pruning the vines when Sheryl suddenly appeared through the rows of vines, crying. When I asked her what the problem was, she told me she was pining for a daughter. The following June, we had our wished-for daughter, Chantelle, completing our family.

Yet, I still wasn't satisfied. I wanted to develop the property so that when I retired, there was enough to sustain both my boys working on the property. Yes, I was a forward planner.

I did some research on rural tourism properties around Australia, such as the Big Banana and Big Pineapple, and discovered there was no working dried fruit property open to the public, not just in Australia but anywhere in the world. So, that became my goal – being the first and only one. I took a notebook up to the block with me every time I went there, and took notes as I thought of ideas for my venture. The only people I told were Sheryl and my family, though my family eventually told me they were sick of hearing me talk about it. With all my plans recorded, I went into action, pulling out vines to make room. Then, once the land was cleared, I built a rubber-tyred train that carried 80 people, and constructed a souvenir shop.

I wanted to open by Christmas 1985 but that didn't happen. However, the property was officially opened to the public on 22 March 1986. I named the business Sultana Sam. In our first year, we had 55,000 visitors and came runner-up in a Victorian Tourism Award.

One day, I recognised one of the visitors. It was Sister Leo. I only had a chance to speak to her briefly but after she had gone, I checked what she had written in the visitors' book: *I loved the tour, John. I knew you could do it.* I was flabbergasted. In Sister Leo's eyes, I had passed. It felt so good.

With so many things on my mind, and so many things to do, I forgot all about Father Day. My depression and nightmares disappeared; I was happy going about my daily life. Unfortunately, Sheryl didn't feel the same way about the property and our life. As I came up with more and more ideas for attractions on the property, and spent time putting them into practice, I was taking Sheryl for granted.

The September school holidays were always busy; some six or seven tours a day, each for an hour. I would be in my element, loving every minute of it. But one day, during those holidays, I got back to the gift shop, where we sold the tour tickets, to find people standing around without tickets and no sign of Sheryl. I ran to the house and asked Chantelle where her mum was.

'In the shop,' she said.

I knew she wasn't, so I found the boys and asked them the same question.

'In the shop,' they said.

I was about to ring the police but decided to call a friend of Sheryl's first, only to be told that Sheryl had left me for one of my mates. Yes, that's how I found out.

I was left with the three children (the youngest just five years old) and a house that soon deteriorated into a mess. My depression and anxiety returned, but I did my best to control them and to keep them hidden from my kids.

The worst of everything was bringing up a young daughter. When you are a victim of abuse, you see and feel it everywhere. The most normal, tender touch becomes abnormal. I found it very difficult washing my daughter and showing her affection. I wouldn't let her climb into my bed in the morning, like she and the boys did when their mother was around. I would have recurring nightmares in which both my daughter and Father Day appeared. This all went on for a couple of years. The day my daughter was old enough to undress and wash herself was one of the happiest days of my life.

A year after leaving me, Sheryl left that so-called mate of mine, returned to Mildura and announced that she wanted to get back with me. I said no, though she did keep in touch with the kids.

One Christmas, Sheryl asked if she could have Chantelle over for a few days, which I agreed to. Our boys went camping with some mates, so I was home alone. My sister invited me over for Christmas Day, but I decided to stay home alone. It was one of the worst decisions I ever made.

I started drinking at about midday on Christmas Day and was still drinking heavily at midnight. I have no idea what happened next but when I woke up in the morning, I found myself sprawled on my bed with a .22 rifle and bullets next to me, and bullet holes in the bedroom ceiling. Staggering into the lounge room, I found more bullets strewn on the floor, two empty bottles of wine, and a slab of empty beer cans. I had never blacked out like that before and it scared me so much. I could so easily have killed myself or, perhaps even worse, ended up in a wheelchair for life. The next day I gave away my guns.

I stepped in and out of a couple of relationships after that but couldn't settle down. I developed insomnia and, to try to shake off the depression, went for long walks through the block in the middle of the night. By 1989, my depression was so bad that I had to employ workers to do my jobs on the block. This was a time of massive interest rates, more than 20%, and with borrowings on my properties, things became financially very tight. This played into my depression, which just got worse and worse. It didn't help that the bank I owed money to was preparing for a public listing. As a result, they put pressure on struggling farmers so that the bank's books looked better for investors.

On 3 January 1990, I had just finished irrigating the property in temperatures in the mid-forties. With some hot, dry north winds, the fruit on the vines were not sugared up enough to harvest, so the irrigation was essential to try to get them to the point where we could pick. But it was futile. While we got the ground wet, it was such a large crop that year that the vines couldn't provide enough moisture for the fruit, and we lost almost the entire year's crop, some fifty tonnes of dried fruit.

For me, that was the last straw. Time to sell and get out. I sold the property but subdivided first, keeping the house on an acre for me.

On 5 March 1991, my dad died from cancer. In some ways, I was glad he died then because he didn't face the sadness of seeing the family property having to be sold. My mum, Amy, lived another seventeen years, dying on 13 November 2008. Her last years were spent in a home and I visited her weekly, or even twice weekly. She never found out what had happened to me at the hands of Father Day. Why didn't I tell them? Mum's faith had something to do with it; I guess I didn't want that crushed. And I was afraid Dad might take matters into his own hands. But really, the main reason was the same as always: I was ashamed and embarrassed.

My boys ended up going their separate ways, one into the air force and the other the army. Chantelle stayed home with me until she was nearly 21 years old, but after she left, none of the kids wanted to know me anymore. Why? I don't know. Maybe because of my anger with the world at the time, or my refusal to take their mother back. Who knows? I now have grandchildren and great grandchildren, so I'm told, but I've only ever seen one of them. That was at my oldest grandchild's baptism, more than two decades ago – and the last time I was invited to anything with my children.

The baptism was at a Sunday mid-morning mass, something I hadn't been to since I was fourteen. Funerals and weddings, sure, with some difficulty, but no masses until that one. I had not even sent my children to a mass, or a Catholic school for that matter. My daughter-in-law and Peter's wife, Pauline, was a Catholic, hence the baptism.

I went to the baptism with my friend, Susan, for support, but as soon as I walked into the church, my sweat glands went berserk. I could feel the moisture on my hands, running from my armpits, behind my knees, just about everywhere. I shivered at the sight of the confessional boxes, and soon teared up. Susan knew something was wrong, but of course, she didn't know what. The only way I was able to calm down was by imagining I was somewhere else, and for me, that was the riverbank.

I sat through the first part of the mass, and then the baptism, but by then I'd had enough. Just getting there and listening to the familiar Catholic homilies had been a struggle. So as people rose to go forth for communion, it seemed the best time to make a quiet exit without anyone noticing. I felt a wave of relief as soon as we stepped outside.

Later that day, I was sitting at the table having a beer when the phone rang. As soon as I picked it up, the verbal tirade started. 'Well, you're a nice piece of work, walking out of the baptism.' It was Pauline. 'You didn't even stay for the reception to meet any of the family.' Then more screaming from her, which I couldn't make sense of, and she slammed the phone down. That was my last contact with any of my children and their families. Of course, Pauline didn't know about my life and my reasons for leaving, which I guess goes to show, you should never make assumptions about someone's actions.

That night, my nightmares returned: confessional boxes, a priest pointing at me, people staring at me. I hardly slept that night.

The next morning, I decided to visit a mate of mine, Kym Burford. I needed to reach out to someone who understood me. He had also been a victim of Father Day. As an altar boy, he had been taken to Melbourne from time to time and housed at Day's sister's home in Williamstown, where Day sexually abused him.

At Kym's house, we made some coffee, then we sat and chatted in his carport. I told him what had happened at the church and the abuse I'd copped, mainly because I wanted to see what his view was. I had started to wonder whether I had done the wrong thing. But I needn't have worried. Kym told me he would have done exactly the same.

'And fuck going into a church,' he said.

I had to agree.

*

At that time, and probably now as well through the equivalent department, the Department of Agriculture and Rural Affairs was providing free counselling for farmers transitioning from the land. After deciding to give it a go, it took me three days to navigate the bureaucracy and make an appointment but finally I found myself in a psychologist's office.

He was young, in his twenties, and as I told him about having to sell the block and my marriage breakdown, he just rooted around in a drawer looking for something. I could tell he wasn't paying much attention. When I had finished, without even telling him about my abuse and school days, he just said, 'Well, in time you will get over it.'

That was it. He was lucky I wasn't feeling too bad that day, and I decided to have fun with the prick. 'Aren't you going to give me a script for some pills?' I said.

'I can't do that. Only a doctor can.'

'So, haven't you got anything else to say to me?'

'What do you want me to say? I'm sorry this has happened to you.'

I'd had enough, so stood to leave. Before I did, I said, 'Well, I know what I want to say. You and the doctors are just educated dickheads.'

And I left, slamming the door behind me. My third attempt at seeking help had been as futile as the first two.

I realised that any help would have to come from within and decided that writing a book about my experiences with Father Day might be cathartic. I began the process by transferring my journal entries from twelve small diaries into one large book. I handwrote every entry, then took the original diaries down the back of the yard and burnt them one at a time, with a beer in hand and a smoke in my mouth. As I watched the pages curling and turning to ash, I felt a sense of satisfaction. I followed every wisp of smoke as it rose and dissipated. I hoped my depression might go with it, but I had wished for that so many times before.

With a disrupted education and leaving school early, writing a book wasn't easy, and I soon put the idea aside, knowing that one day I would come back to it. I got a series of casual jobs and had almost the same number of casual relationships. The latter was not my preference, but I wouldn't allow myself to get too close to the women I became involved with. I guess I didn't want to have to open up about what had happened to me; I was still ashamed. I knew it was Day's fault but there was the added shame of not having said anything, which may have stopped others from being abused.

I often felt that I just needed one person to be able to talk to. A few times I went to call one of my sisters, and even visited them, but chickened out of telling them at the last moment. Of course, the doctors and counsellor I told had been no help, which made me reluctant to seek further assistance that way. And living in a town in Mildura, if I contacted a local health worker, there was every chance I would have known them, which wasn't ideal.

In the early 1990s, the organisation Broken Rites Australia researched Monsignor John Day's activities and in late 1993 released information on Day that was picked up by the media. Even the Mildura *Sunraysia Daily* could not ignore it. Finally, Catholic Church authorities confirmed the Broken Rites revelations and apologised to Day's victims. I read as much as I could about what Broken Rites had uncovered, and Detective Denis Ryan's name cropped up. I remembered him from his time in the police force, and one day built the courage to call him. I explained what had happened to me and he gave me the email address for Broken Rites.

I kept those details for years without doing anything about it. For one thing, I had no idea what an email was. In February 2005, I was talked into buying a computer. I had not even used a typewriter, so a computer was space age stuff to me. It was one hell of a learning curve, but I taught myself how to use it by reading books and asking questions of friends. Just over a year after purchasing the computer, I sent an email to Broken Rites Australia in Melbourne and explained that I was a victim of Father Day. That same day, I received a response from Dr Bernard Barrett, honorary research director for Broken Rites, Melbourne:

Hello John

I am the honorary research director for Broken Rites.

I have been researching Monsignor John Day for the past 13 years. I have talked to several of his victims.

I have written an article about Day. Unfortunately it is not yet on our website. But if you give me your email address, I will send a copy to you.

I have also helped a journalist to write articles in *The Sun Herald* and *The Age* about Day.

Broken Rites can help you to obtain justice. It would be best for you and me to have a chat by phone. If you give me a phone number, I will ring you. As I am a part-time volunteer, I make my Broken Rites phone calls in the evening.

Yes, Broken Rites will respect your privacy and confidentiality. I am the only person who opens this email inbox.

I am a retired academic, specializing in social research. I am interested in helping Broken Rites because I was molested by a De La Salle (Brother Fintan Dwyer at St Bede's DLS College, Mentone) when I was an orphan aged seven. My personal story (with the pseudonym 'Alan') is on the Broken Rites website.

Best wishes,

Dr Bernard Barrett, PhD.

As I read Dr Bernard's letter, I knew I had found the right person at last, and being a victim, he knew what I was talking about.

I sent him my phone number and that night he called. The first thing I asked him was whether he was related to Detective Jim Barritt (I didn't know back then there was a difference in the spelling). Once he had put that concern of mine to bed, we chatted just to get to know each other. After that, whenever I was feeling down, I'd email him. Eventually, he gave me the name of a psychologist, whom I contacted, but my bad luck with counsellors and doctors continued. This one wanted advice on growing vegetables. I now suspect it was a professional way of getting to know the patient and putting them at ease, which made sense, but at the time I just thought he was taking advantage of the fact I had been a farmer. I was impatient and would come away from sessions frustrated. I'd then drive to the river and sit there until I felt ready to drive home.

I let Dr Bernard know that I wasn't happy with the psychologist, and he then recommended an organisation called Towards Healing. I rang the Mildura office and got an answering machine. I left my name and number, then slammed the phone down and yelled, 'You can all get fucked.' I opened a beer and downed it in seconds. I had just wanted to talk to someone.

Just half an hour later, my phone rang. It was a woman named Kerry Buchecker, calling from Towards Healing. We chatted for a while, and I sensed she was different from everyone else I had tried to get help from. When she suggested we meet, I asked that it not be in her office and, to my delight, she agreed. On 25 September 2007, we met over coffee at Centro Shopping Centre, just to get to know each other.

Kerry had met with several other victims of Father Day, so she immediately understood my feelings. We talked for an hour, and every minute, more weight lifted from my shoulders. We spoke for more than an hour and she agreed to meet again away from her office, but this time I asked for somewhere I could have a smoke. We set a time to meet at JC Park by the river, not far from where Judy and I had sat, chatted, fished and read.

At that next meeting, I talked and talked, and that evening, I got an email from Kerry:

> Hi John,
>
> I am saddened to hear of your frustration and despair at what has happened to you. This is of course evidence of the terrible pain that people experience, and often continue to experience as a result of abuse. I can imagine that it is becoming all so more confronting now that you have reached a stage where you are able to talk (albeit very limited) to others about the pain you have experienced over the years.
>
> Take care John, and please be reassured that we will continue to be there for you.
>
> Regards, Kerry

Reading Kerry's email, tears started running down my cheeks. I grabbed a beer but downed it with a completely different attitude to normal. It was not about drinking to get drunk and forget, it was the relief of finding someone to talk to. While Kerry talked about the difficulty in confronting the past, I knew I could do it. The start was hard, but it was the first step in the healing process.

*

My meetings with Kerry helped purge the past and gave me greater insights into myself. I also gained confidence. However, at that stage, outside of doctors and Kym Burford, Kerry was still the only person I had confided in about my childhood; my family didn't know.

The next person I told was someone I started chatting to over the internet in April 2006. We met online through selling various things. Carol was from Gippsland, and she told me about life there, and I told her about Mildura and its dried fruit and wine grape industry. It has never been a romantic connection; she has a loving family, and we have never met in person, nor had a phone call.

On 29 January 2008, I was making notes in preparation for trying to write the book again, so my past was on my mind. That evening, I emailed Carol and told her a tiny bit about my schooldays. There were no details about the abuse, but she picked up on it straight away, replying:

> Are you trying to tell me that a priest abused you as a little boy? I hope to God that isn't so, but if it is, God help him.

I emailed back:

> Yes that's what happened.

Another barrier had fallen. I had told someone who wasn't a professional. Carol's fury led her to state, 'Kids are the most precious beings on this earth.'

They so are. They are our future on this planet, and they need to be watched over and protected from vermin creatures, so their childhood is not ripped from them. Losing one's childhood through sexual abuse has a bearing on the rest of one's life. Through my research, I have found that many end up homeless, living as hermits on riverbanks, in sheds, under bridges, on the streets. I was lucky that I didn't end up like that, but I was a victim in many other ways, and I hurt many people I loved because of my inability to cope. However, with the right people walking beside me, the likes of Kerry and Carol, the light that went out at the end of that very dark tunnel will return and get brighter, and I will be able to walk out the other end a better person.

My meetings with Kerry progressed from the park to her office as I got more comfortable with her. At one meeting, we decided to walk from her office to Scared Heart Primary School, the church, and the presbytery. I felt great apprehension but went through with it. Walking though the school grounds, everything had changed so much. After all, it had been more than fifty years since I was there. I didn't feel anything until we got to the presbytery, which looked the same, and hatred stirred inside me.

Having gotten so many things off my chest, and having Kerry and Carol as supporters, I was again ready to start writing my book. It proved bloody hard work. There wasn't a chapter that didn't bring memories flooding back. There wasn't a chapter that didn't see me take a break, go for a walk and clear my head. There wasn't a chapter that didn't involve tears and thoughts of other children going through the same nightmares.

In writing the book, I decided to track some people down and talk to them. One was Anna, who I had seen from time to time over the years, usually in the local supermarket. I waited at the supermarket checkouts several times, for hours, finally seeing her buying her groceries. As she passed, I said, 'Hi Anna.'

She was a little uneasy because I was standing there, at the checkout, with no groceries. Her eyes were sad, and her face had stress lines, but finally she replied, nervously, 'Oh, hi. John, isn't it?'

I asked if I could buy her a coffee but she turned me down flat. 'Anna, I need your help,' I said. 'I'm writing a book about my school days and …'

She cut me short. 'School days? Not likely.' She started to walk away.

'Please Anna. I need your help, to help others.'

She ignored me and I watched her walk out of the shopping centre. I wasn't going to chase her. She had every right to ignore me. I walked in the opposite direction, towards another exit, until I heard a voice behind me.

'John. John.' It was Anna. 'I will have that coffee with you.'

We went to the nearest coffee shop and sat down. She asked what I wanted from her and I said, 'I don't know where to start, Anna, but I remember when we were at school and going to church, quite often I would see you crying. I know you live on your own and don't go out much and I was wondering ...'

'It's none of your business,' she snapped.

She started to get up and gave me a look to kill. I knew I had stuffed up and said it all wrong. I had to say something fast. 'Please sit down, Anna. I was a victim of Day and I just wanted to talk to you. Please.'

She flopped into her seat like a rag doll and stared at me, her eyes filling with tears. 'John, I'm sorry,' she said, 'but I can't talk to you here.'

'Tell me when and where and I'll be there.'

'No, give me your number and I'll call you.'

As I wrote my number on a piece of paper, I could see Anna's hands clutching her handbag, her knuckles turning white. I passed the paper to her and she left without saying another word. It was two weeks before she called, and we arranged to meet at the same place. I got there half an hour early, figuring I'd need that time to think what to say to her. Unfortunately, she arrived fifteen minutes early, so I only had half the time I had expected.

Anna sat down with an icy look on her face, as if she'd rather be anywhere else. 'So, you were assaulted by Father Day,' she said.

'Yes,'

'Same.' There was silence, before she added, 'And I don't have time for a coffee.'

I told her that I used to see her crying on the way to church, and that I could put her in touch with people who could help her, even now.

She just said, 'No,' stood up and left. I have not seen her since.

In early February 2008, I was sitting in Kerry's office when she told me, 'I have some good news for you, John. The Bishop of Ballarat, Peter Connors, will be here in a couple of weeks to say sorry to you on behalf of the Church.'

I was flabbergasted. I didn't know what to say. After more than fifty years someone was going to say sorry. It seemed like a dream.

Kerry told me that a meeting place had to be set up, and that a mediator, Shane Wall, would be up a week beforehand to brief me on what would occur, and to represent me at the meeting with the bishop. I told Kerry that I didn't want to speak to the bishop, as I hadn't been near a priest for years, let alone a bishop.

'You won't have to,' she told me. 'We have all the documentation we need and we have your statement. Shane Wall and I will talk for you.'

And so, the following week, I met with Shane and Kerry in preparation for the meeting with Bishop Peter Connors.

I got postcards printed to promote Sultana Sam. This one shows me loading grapes onto the drying racks.

The front cover of a book I produced on Sultana Sam.

A photo of me promoting the book.

THE HEALING PROCESS

The twin hosts of the Channel Seven kids' show, Wombat, came to visit Sultana Sam to record a story on my dried fruit business and tourism venture.

The common practice to prepare the grapes for drying was to dip them into a tank first. But I invented a machine that sprayed them on the racks. Here I am supervising the spraying.

At home with Chantelle (age four).

Chantelle's fourth birthday.

CHAPTER TWELVE

THE APOLOGY

Nine days before I received my apology, Prime Minister Kevin Rudd stood up in Parliament and delivered an apology to the Indigenous Stolen Generations on behalf of the nation. The director of the National Centre for Indigenous Studies, Professor Mick Dodson, referred to the apology as 'the corner piece of a jigsaw puzzle – the rock to build the future'.

Dodson's words resonated with me, as I prepared for my apology on 22 February 2008. After fifty years of searching for a building block to start again, this was an opportunity to see life in a different way, and to recognise that there are people out there who care about making the world a better, safer place, particularly for kids. However, I was under no illusion that the apology was a magic fix. There would be a hell of a lot more of the jigsaw to put together. Still, you need to start with the first piece.

The previous few years, I'd chosen to live on my own. I'd become somewhat of a hermit, but happy with my own company. Several times, they'd be a knock on my door and I would peek through the curtains. If I didn't know them, the door stayed closed. Even if I did know them, many times I wouldn't answer. Father Day was responsible for that. The impact of that monster is still around decades after his abuse. Despite his death, it rears its ugly head without warning or reason.

One day I was in Adelaide with my then partner. We were in a shopping centre when there was an announcement over the intercom that a little girl was lost. They described what she was wearing and it matched a girl wandering in our aisle. Without thinking, I took her hand and led her to the checkout. The girl's mother saw me and gave me a look I will never forget. Most men would have explained the situation and laughed it off. But I couldn't do either. That event caused me great distress, to the point that I try not to have anything to do with children.

One of my fears in telling others of the abuse I suffered is that many victims of abuse grow up to display anti-social behaviour, even abusing others. It's common knowledge, and I fear I will be viewed in that way. A 1986 study of male adolescent sexual abuse survivors published in the *Psychological Bulletin* indicated that more than 80% had histories of substance abuse, 50% had suicidal thoughts, 23% attempted suicide and almost 70% received psychological treatment. Survivors are also more prone to adult criminal behaviour, according to two studies published by the National Institute of Justice.

Despite that, institutions within which abuse occurred – such as the Catholic Church, but others as well – spent decades protecting abusers and covering up their crimes. Thousands and thousands of lives have been ruined, not just the victims' lives but their families as well. They may be statistics in the paragraph above but they represent real people. People like me.

At 12.30 on 22 February 2008, I met Kerry in a coffee shop near the mall. Kerry had chosen it because it had an outdoor area and she knew I liked to smoke. As I rolled my cigarette, I looked around as I always did, anxious to hide my face from anyone who might have known me. In my view, being seen with a psychologist could be taken as a sign of weakness. I'd done it so many times, Kerry now laughed and said, 'Don't worry, we could be having a business meeting.'

The meeting with Bishop Peter Connors was to take place at 2 pm at the Mildura RSL Club. The catch-up with Kerry was to calm my nerves beforehand. Over coffee, Kerry looked at her watch and said, 'Not long now, John.'

After waiting fifty years, it certainly wasn't long to go. It seemed like a dream.

Kerry assured me that there was nothing to be nervous about. This wasn't an inquisition. 'Bishop Connors is a very understanding man,' she said. 'He is very aware of what went on with Father Day in this area. You won't have to talk about anything that happened. He has plenty of notes that we've provided him with.'

I found that a huge relief. I really didn't want to talk to him.

For another hour, we talked about anything and everything but Father Day and the upcoming meeting. Finally, it was time to get going. My heart started to race.

I drove there by myself. More than once I had an overwhelming feeling to turn around and drive home. It was all so surreal. After fifty years of waiting, someone was going to listen to me, or at least to those speaking on my behalf. Tears filled my eyes. I pulled up in the RSL carpark and wiped the tears away, just as I saw Kerry approaching my car.

We walked into the club together and the young woman at the front desk said, 'The Bishop and Mr Wall are in the meeting room now.'

My heart skipped a beat. Did she know why I was there?

Walking towards the meeting room reminded me of the many walks to the confession box. After all, there was a priest behind that door. Kerry went in first. I was very apprehensive about entering, but Kerry gave me time, holding the door open for me until I was ready. Shane Wall was sitting at one end of a table and Bishop Connors was sitting next to him.

Shane stood up and introduced me to Bishop Connors. The bishop put out his hand and I shook it. He was older than I expected but clearly alert and full of energy. I couldn't look him in the eye, and every time he looked at me, I turned away. He must have noticed because he stopped looking at me, and started looking down at the table, almost as if he was praying. He was dressed in normal clothes, a cross below his left shoulder the only sign of his calling.

Shane started proceedings, explaining that we were there for the Church to acknowledge that Father Day had sexually assaulted me, and then gave a statement to the bishop, providing some details of the abuse.

Then Kerry had her say, explaining our relationship and our regular meetings; she even read an email from me to her about my life as a victim of abuse, and how things got better as we had gotten to know each other. As she spoke, I couldn't stop the tears from running down my face. I was overwhelmed by the way she was speaking of me. As I wrote in an email to her that night, 'I've never come across anyone the likes of you before, you were so caring.' There is no doubt, I would never have been able to have the meeting with Bishop Connors without Kerry.

When Kerry had finished, Bishop Connors had his say. He told me how the Catholic Church was deeply sorry this had happened, and that they had proof that Monsignor John Day had sexually assaulted children. They had removed a plaque with Day's name that had been mounted on a church. He also explained that the Church had introduced processes whereby priests were now not allowed to be alone with children, even altar boys, or taken alone to a presbytery like I had. Finally, he told me he knew that my sister, Pat, was a devoted nun and doing great work for the order, and that he would like my permission to speak to her and Marlene for me.

Those last few words broke me up, as I realised my family now needed to be told. I didn't respond straight away. I looked to Kerry, who was also wiping tears off her cheeks.

'Yes, please, I would like that. I'm too gutless to do it myself. I can't tell them on my own, it's gone on too long, fifty years too long.'

'No John, you're not gutless,' Bishop Connors said. 'It's taken a lot of courage to get this far. We will provide on-going help and support for you from now on.' Then came maybe the best of all. 'And also, a letter of apology written to you from the Church, would you like that?'

'Yes, I would.'

The meeting came to end, with the bishop's final words being, 'John, on behalf of the Church we are very sorry. We are sincerely sorry this has happened to you.'

I shook hands with Shane and Bishop Connors and turned to Kerry. We gave each other a hug, crying as we did. 'Thank you, Kerry,' I whispered.

*

With the apology from the Church delivered, it was time for my family to be told. I didn't want them to hear about it second-hand, but it was going to have to wait until Bishop Connors could come up again, which he had said would be about three months.

About a fortnight after the apology, I started getting anxiety attacks and nightmares. I knew they were related to having to tell my family. In my nightmares, my sisters were yelling at me, and my children were walking away from me, then turning back with disgusted looks on their faces. After four nights in a row of this recurring nightmare, I decided I had to tell them as soon as possible. I rang Kerry and we made a time to meet the following day, but on that next morning, I rang and cancelled, making an excuse that something had come up.

In the period waiting for Bishop Connors to return to Mildura, I had regular sessions with Kerry. She helped me through my anxieties as best she could. Finally, the date was set for the meeting with my sisters: 30 May 2008, in Mildura.

A few days before the scheduled meeting, I sent an email to Kerry explaining that I didn't want to hurt my sisters and I didn't know why I had started all this. I wrote that I felt scared of facing my sisters after they had been told. On receiving the email, Kerry rang and said she would speak to me in the morning.

I waited for the call, but it didn't come until mid-afternoon. Kerry told me to go straight to her office. When I got there, she looked concerned, and told me, 'A few things have happened today.' I tried to imagine what it could have been, but she quickly came out with it. 'I hope you won't be mad with me,' she said. 'But I saw your sisters today and told them. And it all went well.'

I sat in silence, totally dumbfounded. I couldn't believe what I was hearing. Finally, I spoke. 'How are they?'

'They're fine. Upset and sorry for you, but fine. And they would like to see you.'

Again, I sat and gathered my thoughts. Then I told Kerry that I wanted to be alone that night but would see them the next afternoon.

Kerry said she would let them know, then told me that the bishop would still meet with my sisters the upcoming Saturday morning.

Driving home, I couldn't believe it was over, at least in terms of telling my sisters about the abuse. While what Kerry had done may have been a bit unethical, she had done it because of my email to her. She knew I couldn't take the stress any longer. And, after all those years worrying about what my sisters would say or do, they turned out to be understanding and supportive, and we have remained close.

In talking to people and doing some research, I found out many things about the abuse children suffered at the hands of Father Day. For example, he used to drive young girls around in his Pontiac, and on one occasion he insisted the girl sitting next to him take over the steering wheel. When she did, he accelerated to around 120 km/h and whispered in her ear to keep both hands firmly on the wheel or they would crash and both die. He then put his hands inside her pants and assaulted her. I also discovered that while I was at school, being abused by Day, other students knew what he was like. When they saw him in the playground, they would sing a ditty: 'Bums to the ground, Pappy's around.' Because I stopped mixing with the children and skipped school a lot, I never heard it.

Of course, if the children knew, adults had to know as well. And they did. John Howden, deputy principal of St Joseph's College, wrote a letter to Father Day's bishop, Ronald Mulkearns, advising him of the allegations and asking him to remove Day before he abused more victims. Not only did Mulkearns not respond to Howden, but he also sent a letter to all parishioners urging them to stick by their priests and ignore any rumours they might hear.

Not all the priests protected Day, or his reputation after Day's death. On 4 July 1997, Mildura parish priest Patrick Mugavin issued a circular admitting there was evidence to support claims that Day had sexually assaulted children. He wrote:

> Personally, I have no doubt as to what took place. I would like to offer a sincere apology to victims on the behalf of the Church and seek their forgiveness for what happened in the past. There is deep-seated shock and hurt within the parish, particularly when trust is betrayed by a church leader.
>
> It seems there is substance to such allegations, although, unfortunately, they were never judged by a court of law.
>
> As a church we offer our sincere apology to any victims and deeply regret the hurt and pain that has been caused. If the response of the Church authorities was perceived not to have been adequate, we express regret and sorrow.

Contemplating life in my fifties.

CHAPTER THIRTEEN

FRUSTRATION

As important as the apology was to me, it did not end my pain and frustration. My frustrations were spread far and wide, but particularly to the Church and Victoria Police. On the afternoon of Sunday 30 June 2019, I sat at my computer and composed an email to the complaints department at Victoria Police. It read:

Dear Sir/Madam,

This complaint is back in the late 1950s and 1960s in Mildura. I am a victim of Father John Day for two years, a lot of this history is written in newspapers, and a book that X Detective Denis Ryan has written. I have a chapter in this book plus photo, (my story is page 227) the book is called 'Unholy Trinity' that Denis has written.

Myself I've gone through a lot after those early days as a child it's been hard, a lot of people in those days knew what was going on, including the Mildura Police Force and the Victoria Chief Commissioner of police of the day. The editor of our local paper (*Sunraysia Daily*) George Tilley wouldn't allow his reporters go near Fr John Day yet they had known what he was up to of course he was Catholic like most of the police back then.

There's a lot written on this so there's no need for me to go through this, in the book and newspapers also Broken Rites. I don't want to take anything away from Denis Ryan he done a great job and I know him very well and still see him. What I want to know how come the Police Department gave Denis and apology and payout when the victims in Mildura had nothing from the police, if police had done their job in Mildura a lot of children plus myself wouldn't have gone through sexual abuse by Fr John Day or Detective Jim Barritt that run this town back then it was frightening days back then as a kid I was scared every day. I've written to police before about this but got nothing just some bullshit seeing someone, well I've been going to a psychologist for a lot of years so don't tell me about that again, I want something done. I now have a solicitor in Melbourne and they have gone to a QC about the Mildura Police back then.

It would be great if this letter was shown to Graham Ashton (Chief Commissioner) but I dare say I've got Buckley's and none of that happen, I don't think you the reader have no idea what we victims go through. But I'm not going away, the police have already had a write up in our paper and locals are not happy. Even doing this letter it's hard for me, I've had to walk away every now and then. PLEASE Please listen to US.

John Fitzgibbon

Two days later I received the following reply:

> Hi John
>
> I remember when your matter came through via IBAC just over 3 years ago. You spoke to a Sgt at Mildura and you were also referred to Task Force Sano.
>
> I agree entirely with your comments that no person has an idea of what victims went through in the 50s and 60s and the ever lasting impact on their lives.
>
> Denis Ryan received an apology and payout as he was an employee of Victoria Police who had his career ruined for trying to stand up for good against evil.
>
> The Chief Commissioner has publicly apologised for the failings of Victoria Police.
>
> I appreciate you are seeing a psychologist for years so I won't offer any referral services.
>
> Regards
>
> **Andrew Gates**
> *Acting Senior Sergeant 27811*
> *Police Conduct Unit*
> *Professional Standards Command*

And that was that, for me and all the victims.

From left: Denis Ryan, me, and Kym Burford. The Church and the Victoria Police have a lot to answer for, to the three of us.

CHAPTER FOURTEEN

GETTING ON WITH LIFE

Before I spoke up – before people learnt what had happened to me – I felt paralysed. I hid my depression and my thoughts. I was like an actor taking on a different character. Deep inside, though, I was hurting real bad. Getting it all out was like releasing the valve on a pressure cooker.

Sure, I still feel lost sometimes, but I have improved a hell of a lot. It's thanks to the people around me; I now know they would have supported me all along. It was a huge shock for them. I had lived with it for more than fifty years, but they had no idea. Of course, there are some people, people very close to me, who have nothing to do with me anymore. That's their choice. I have to get on with my life.

What's that life look like? I spend most of my time on the river on a houseboat, having sold the house I built for my family, after losing all interest in the hard work I'd put into it.

I also sold a lot of my possessions and gave others away. I kept only a few items I needed. I still have a small, isolated property but I spend most of my time on my boat on the Murray River, and taking my two German shepherds for walks in the bush. And I'm still getting counselling.

Writing my story was hard. It took a long time. Many times I had to walk away from it because it caused enormous emotional pain. But I'm glad I did it, and it has helped a lot. Maybe it's my way of making up for keeping quiet when I was younger. Maybe someone reading it will recognise elements of their own experiences and take the steps that took me decades. I hope so. I often wonder how

I lived through it all, but I did. Now I'm glad I did, so I can tell my story. So I can get on with my life.

Me, in 2023, contemplating on the bank of the Murray, where I spend time alone in my thoughts – and with Judy, from all those years ago.

www.ingramcontent.com/pod-product-compliance
Lightning Source LLC
Chambersburg PA
CBHW040243130526
44591CB00039B/2831